KNOXVILLE

Smoky Mountain Majesty

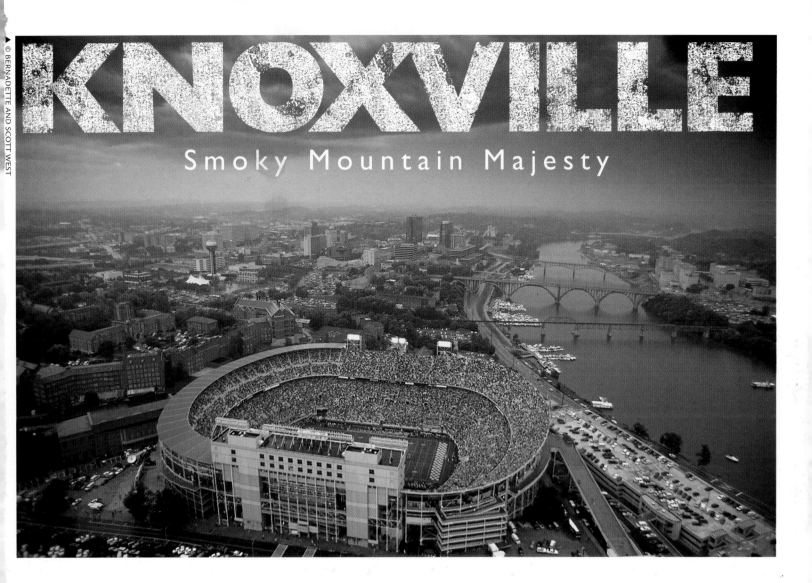

KNOXVILLE

Smoky Mountain Majesty

Introduction by
Howard H. Baker Jr.

Art Direction by
Bob Kimball

Sponsored by the
Knoxville Area
Chamber Partnership

Knoxville

KNOXVILLE
Smoky Mountain Majesty

Contents

URBAN
TAPESTRY
SERIES
TOWERY
PUBLISHING, INC.

By Howard H. Baker Jr.

The most famous thing ever said about Knoxville was a lie.

In his widely read work *Inside U.S.A.*, published in 1946, traveler-author John Gunther called Knoxville "the ugliest city I ever saw in America, with the exception of a few small mill towns in New England."

Today, decades later, Gunther's scathing—and ill-informed—attack on the city continues to evoke stinging rebuttal from those who know the city best—expletives that one local historian described as "usually reserved for Democrats and the unchurched."

For Knoxville natives—and the more than 9 million visitors who trek through the East Tennessee mountains and countryside each year—it's easy to dismiss Gunther's assessment as the misguided ramblings of a confused traveler who had been away from home one too many nights.

After all, we know better.

Knoxville is, in fact, a city of rare beauty that manifests itself uniquely in every season. Its magnificence is showcased in thousands of blooming dogwoods each spring; in the brightly colored boat sails on its vast, shimmering lakes in the summer; in the burning red and orange of the leaves of autumn; and in the snowcapped peaks of nearby Clingman's Dome and Mount LeConte—majestic summits that capture the last glimmer of sun as the light dies in winter.

In addition to its physical beauty, Knoxville is appealing in other ways as well. It was here, as a youth, that I was first introduced to the rough-and-tumble world of politics—a world that would become my life and my passion. I was mesmerized and forever changed as I watched performances by some of the most colorful players on the stage of local government anywhere. Knoxville, a wag once noted, is a city where "the girls are the grandest and the politics the damnedest." This statement, unlike Gunther's, is absolutely true. ▶

Two of my earliest—though unwitting—tutors in the civics drama class that is local government were Cas Walker and George Dempster. I—along with many other East Tennesseans—gleefully watched the verbal sparring of Cas and George from afar the way kids today pack arenas to see Rocky "The Rock" Maivia or "Stone Cold" Steve Austin. Even in the days before media coverage was so intense, Cas and George were characters worthy of any WWF match. Both were millionaires. Both had a fierce and loyal following. And, being politicians, both were opinionated and vocal. Like The Rock and Stone Cold, they often found themselves—sometimes loudly—on opposite sides of an issue.

Cas Walker was a successful grocery man who hosted a local television show. His program aired at 6 a.m. each weekday and provided an early catalyst for the careers of various musical talents—including Dolly Parton, who began her meteoric rise in country music on *The Cas Walker Show*. George Dempster, a former Knoxville mayor, was the inventor (along with his brothers) of the ubiquitous Dempster Dumpster, now a permanent feature of the nation's landscape as the preferred method of portable waste disposal.

Walker and Dempster were perennial adversaries, who engaged in unending political squabbles that were at once acrimonious and amusing. George probably characterized the feelings of both men at one point when he told a friend: "If I ordered a carload of SOBs, and they just sent me Cas, I'd sign for the whole shipment."

From my earliest memory, I was enthralled by politics and politicians. U.S. Congressman J. Will Taylor of LaFollette was the first congressman I ever saw. He stayed overnight in our home when I was five or six years old. He drove a large Studebaker and wore a corset. I don't know which impressed me most: Congress, the car, or the corset. In later life, I had a closer, firsthand look at politics as various members of my family held both local and federal posts, serving the citizens of Knox County and the surrounding region. My father, Howard Baker Sr., served seven terms in the U.S. House of Representatives. My stepmother, Irene Baker,

finished out his final term in Congress following his death in 1964, and later served as Knoxville's public welfare director from 1965 to 1971.

Undoubtedly, though, my most colorful political relative was my maternal grand-mother. Her name was Lilly Ladd. We called her Mother Ladd. As sheriff of neighboring Roane County in the 1920s, Mother Ladd was a major early influence in my political life. I was probably 12 years old before I realized that all grandmothers don't sleep with a nickel-plated, .32-caliber pistol under their pillow.

As officeholders, my family members set a good example for me. They were all compassionate people, sensitive to the needs of the citizens they served. I learned much from observing their character and behavior. Most of all, I learned that the essence of public service is to be an advocate—to speak when it matters most for those who otherwise might have no voice. My family's experience and insight helped shape my perspective as I later moved onto the national stage as a U.S. Senator, majority leader, White House Chief of Staff, and presidential candidate.

They say "all politics is local." I couldn't agree more. My East Tennessee experience taught me that every national issue has local roots and a local point of view that must be considered and factored into the final outcome. While everyone will not be satisfied with the result, each has a right to his say. We all agree to abide by the decision of the majority. That is the beauty of our representative democracy.

Today, Knoxville is blessed with progressive political leadership, a healthy business climate, respect for the risk-taking entrepreneur, a record of unparalleled achievement in technology and innovation, and an appreciation of the global economy that marks our entry into the exciting 21st century.

The more I have had the opportunity to see and learn about the rest of our great country, the more I have come to know that Gunther was wrong about my hometown. As I dealt with issues of world trade and the national economy during my years in government, I came to appreciate even more the strength and beauty of Knoxville as an economic competitor and a beautiful place to do business. ▶

Knoxville is located in the geographical center of the eastern United States and is within a day's drive of half the nation's population. Literally in the center of the action, the city is situated at the crossroads of three major interstates—I-75, I-40, and I-81—and sits on the banks of the Tennessee River, which connects the city to major U.S. ports.

Knoxville is also the center of the thriving eastern region of Tennessee and is a year-round destination for travelers. The city is surrounded by three national parks, including the Great Smoky Mountains National Park, the most visited in the nation, attracting nearly 10 million visitors per year. On the other side of Knoxville from the Smokies is the Big South Fork National Recreation Area. Big South Fork had 1 million visitors in 2000, and may be growing faster than we locals would like.

Along with the spectacular mountain ranges, the so-called Great Lakes of the South—dozens of glistening lakes that surround Knoxville—provide easily accessible sports and recreation opportunities, which are enjoyed by thousands of residents and visitors each year. Many of these lakes are man-made, created as part of the highly successful flood control and rural electrification program undertaken by the Tennessee Valley Authority (TVA)—itself one of the great experiments of American democracy.

Two years before Gunther raised the ire of Knoxvillians, one of the TVA's first directors, David Lilienthal, wrote a much more glowing review of the region, its resources, and the strength of its inhabitants. He described TVA as the story of "a wandering and inconstant river now become a chain of broad and lovely lakes." People enjoy the lakes, he said, "on which they can depend, in all seasons, for movement of the barges of commerce that nourish their business enterprises."

Lilienthal wrote powerfully of TVA as the story of "how waters once wasted and destructive have been controlled and now work, night and day, creating electric energy to lighten the burden of human drudgery."

Lilienthal called TVA "a tale of fields grown old and barren with the years which now are vigorous with new fertility, lying green to the sun; of forests that were

hacked and despoiled, now protected and refreshed with strong young trees just starting on their slow road to maturity."

And, most important, Lilienthal concluded, TVA is the story of the people and how they worked together to create a new valley and, ultimately, a new South.

The New South, a phrase first coined by Atlanta editor Henry Grady, is as much about an attitude as a place. The New South was a hopeful concept, an optimistic celebration of possibilities, rising out of the ashes of Confederate defeat, vigorously embracing the modern industrial age. In the New South's economy, agriculture—for decades a mainstay of prosperity and lifestyle—began to fade in favor of industrialization, urbanization, and economic diversification.

Grady was eloquent in his description of a painful but inevitable transition that sought to blend the region's rich heritage with its indomitable spirit and thirst for economic prosperity. "Never was nobler duty confided to human hands," he wrote, "than the uplifting and upbuilding of the prostrate and bleeding South— misguided perhaps, but beautiful in her suffering."

Knoxville was—and remains today—a progressive, charter member of the New South movement, a city proud of her heritage, rich in imagination, dedicated to innovation, and standing watch at the outposts of learning—searching expectantly for tomorrow's brightest ideas.

Like other southern cities that blossomed into national prominence as Americans embraced the economy and lifestyle of the Sun Belt, Knoxville has come a long way. The city and the state as a whole have, thankfully, left behind the post-Civil War century. Tennesseans today are worried more about our grandchildren than about our grandfathers.

Local historians William Bruce Wheeler and Michael McDonald note that, at the outset of the Civil War, Knoxville was a "modest town that had served successively as a speculative venture, a seat of government, a way station through which

travelers headed West would pass, a small commercial center, and one of several towns on the railroad lines that linked the South with the more dynamic regions of the North and West."

Today, Knoxville is no longer a stop on the road to somewhere else. It is a destination in its own right. The city has become a magnet for tourists, the arts, science and technology, sports, recreation, entrepreneurship, and almost everything else that adds to prosperity, opportunity, and the enjoyment of life.

In particular, the Knoxville area has developed a strong international reputation for innovation and technology development through the joint efforts of the University of Tennessee (UT), TVA, and the federal energy research and development facilities located in nearby Oak Ridge.

Oak Ridge is an integral part of America's history, having played a central role in the successful Manhattan Project that produced the first atomic bomb that led to the end of World War II. Today, the Oak Ridge facilities, operated by the U.S. Department of Energy, remain key elements of America's strong national defense and our efforts to unlock even more secrets of nature. Oak Ridge scientists are making important inroads in areas ranging from our ability to diagnose and treat disease to new ways to clean up contamination, protect our environment, increase food supplies, and produce new energy sources for the future.

Research in all three of these organizations—UT, Oak Ridge, and TVA—has spawned dozens of successful entrepreneurial spin-offs, which in turn have created hundreds of new jobs and added to the region's reputation for technological leadership. To further promote the area's international image in technology, local leaders have created Tennessee's Resource Valley, which packages the capabilities of public and private organizations to recruit new technological ventures to the region.

The strong research and development focus at Oak Ridge is enhanced by the close working relationship between the University of Tennessee, which has its main campus in Knoxville, and Oak Ridge National Laboratory (ORNL), one of the nation's leading federal research institutions. ▶

Chartered in 1794, UT now has a total enrollment of more than 26,000 and an annual research budget of more than $75 million. Today's campus, with its sprawling classroom complexes, sophisticated laboratories, and mammoth, 107,000-seat football stadium, would be a sight to behold for William Blount, governor of the territories south of the Ohio River—land that was to become the state of Tennessee.

A former North Carolina soldier who crossed the mountains as part of America's westward expansion, Blount was a visionary who, as governor, presided over the chartering of the university. He insisted that UT be coeducational because he wanted his daughter and her friends to attend. Succumbing to the culture of the times, the university didn't stay coed long, but thanks to Blount's vision and insistence, it started out that way.

We're all glad UT eventually got back to its coed roots. UT women graduates have excelled in all fields of endeavor, from business to science and the arts—even space exploration. UT women have also distinguished themselves in college athletics, as the Lady Vols basketball team consistently dominates its sport, boasting top-ranked players and repeat national championships.

And, as the T-shirts on campus say, the Vols also "play a little football," fielding a team that is, predictably, often ranked in the nation's top 10 and one that earned national championship status in the 1998 season.

The Baker family roots run deep at the University of Tennessee. When our grandson, Daniel Baker, entered UT as a freshman in 2000, he became the fifth-generation Baker to attend. While I don't envy him having to make some of the difficult, life-altering decisions I faced as a young student years ago, I hope his decision-making process is as at least as thoughtful as mine was.

It is still vivid in my recollection that my decision to enter a life in the law was predicated on nothing more profound than the fact that the line to register in law school was shorter than the line for engineering school. For a young man returning home from the navy after World War II, a shorter line was all the career encouragement I needed! ▶

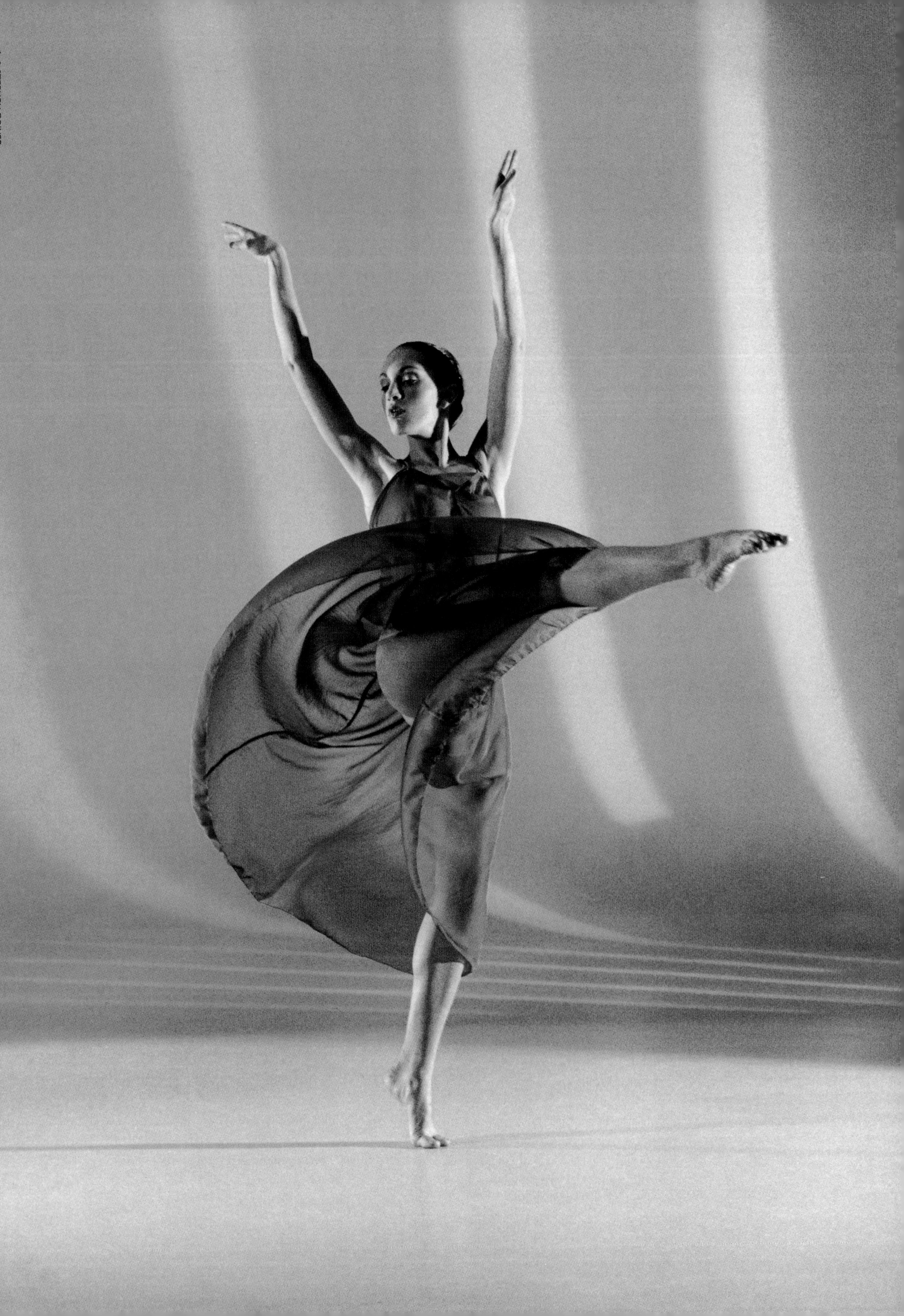

© STEPHEN DRIVER

But I—as I'm sure Daniel will, too—found plenty of real career encouragement at the University of Tennessee. It is a place that fosters excellence, provides a platform for success, and expands our desire and ability to make the world around us a better place.

As UT moves into its third century, the university is flourishing amid growing partnerships at home and abroad. As an example, the UT/ORNL Science Alliance has been established to maximize the scientific resources of both UT and the government facilities at nearby Oak Ridge. The Science Alliance has a twofold mission: to promote collaboration between ORNL and UT, and to improve selected science programs at the University of Tennessee.

The Science Alliance's mission is accomplished through several avenues, including a Distinguished Scientist Program, a Collaborating Scientist Program, the Science Alliance Faculty Research Awards, and joint institutes that bring talented people together from around the globe.

The international involvement promoted by the Science Alliance is but one example of the cosmopolitan nature of the region, which promotes learning, cultural exchange, and outreach to many nations of the world. While continually celebrating their native salt-of-the-earth Appalachian roots, Knoxvillians have adopted an increasingly sophisticated outlook, reaching out to embrace the diverse cultural riches of the nation and the world at large.

The Knoxville Museum of Art serves as a permanent repository for artistic treasures, as well as a way station for itinerant cultural assets that give East

Tennesseans a glimpse of life in other times and faraway places. In addition to its growing collection of American contemporary art, the museum has hosted more than 120 traveling exhibits since 1990.

Faced and surrounded with Tennessee pink marble, the modular-shaped Knoxville Museum of Art moved in 1990 to World's Fair Park, site of the 1982 World's Fair, and near the inner-city skyline. Celebrated New York museum architect Edward Larabee Barnes designed the 53,000-square-foot building, which contains 12,700 square feet of exhibit space in five galleries. Other features include a Great Hall with a panoramic view of the city and a 170-seat auditorium, which hosts numerous meetings and groups each year.

Dolly Parton is but one of the well-known country music stars who began their careers in Knoxville. In fact, had it not been for a single, overwhelming asset based in Nashville—clear channel radio station WSM 650 with its powerful AM signal, which was able to reach out to much of the country—Knoxville would today probably be known as the Country Music Capital of the World.

In addition to Dolly, who grew up in nearby Sevierville, Knoxville's country music heroes include the Everly Brothers (who attended Knoxville's West High School), Roy Acuff, Archie Campbell, and many others. Singer-songwriter Don Gibson penned one of country's greatest hits, "Sea of Heartbreak," in the 1950s while living in a trailer park on Clinton Highway in north Knox County.

Although Dolly was fortunate enough to be East Tennessean by birth, as was I, many others have adopted the rugged mountains, friendly culture, and easy lifestyle of the Knoxville region as their permanent home. These natives-by-choice have influenced millions in America and around the world through their contributions to science, technology, government, and the arts.

One such transplant was Alex Haley.

Author of the best-selling, culture-defining book *Roots*, Haley was a native of Henning in West Tennessee. The famed African-American storyteller spent the last

14 years of his life in East Tennessee, specifically adopting Knoxville as his home. Today, a 13-foot, bronze statue of Haley sits on a Knoxville hillside in an area known as Haley Heritage Square. Haley's image is directed toward the Smoky Mountains that he loved. Dressed casually, he holds a copy of *Roots*. Haley is emblematic of those who could have chosen to live anywhere and found a home in Knoxville. In so doing, they enriched the region by their presence and enduring works.

Though I have had the good fortune to visit most of America's towns and cities, and have stood in awe at the splendor of the world's great capitals, I have never really been far from Knoxville.

To me, Knoxville is more than a city.

It is a personal experience—one that touches all the senses and evokes the deepest memories and best hopes. It is the high energy of commerce, manufacturing, and technology. The thrill of invention and innovation. The smell of freshly plowed soil, fertile and rich, yielding the earth's fruits.

It is the eagle soaring in breathless beauty above a mountain peak. The serenity of a sunrise over a shining lake. The rushing, mighty sound of victory on a football Saturday in Neyland Stadium.

These are the sights and sounds that are forever with me. Wherever I am, Knoxville is always calling me back home. It is a voice I will always hear—and one my heart has chosen to heed.

If only John Gunther could see us now. ▪

▲ © BERNADETTE AND SCOTT WEST

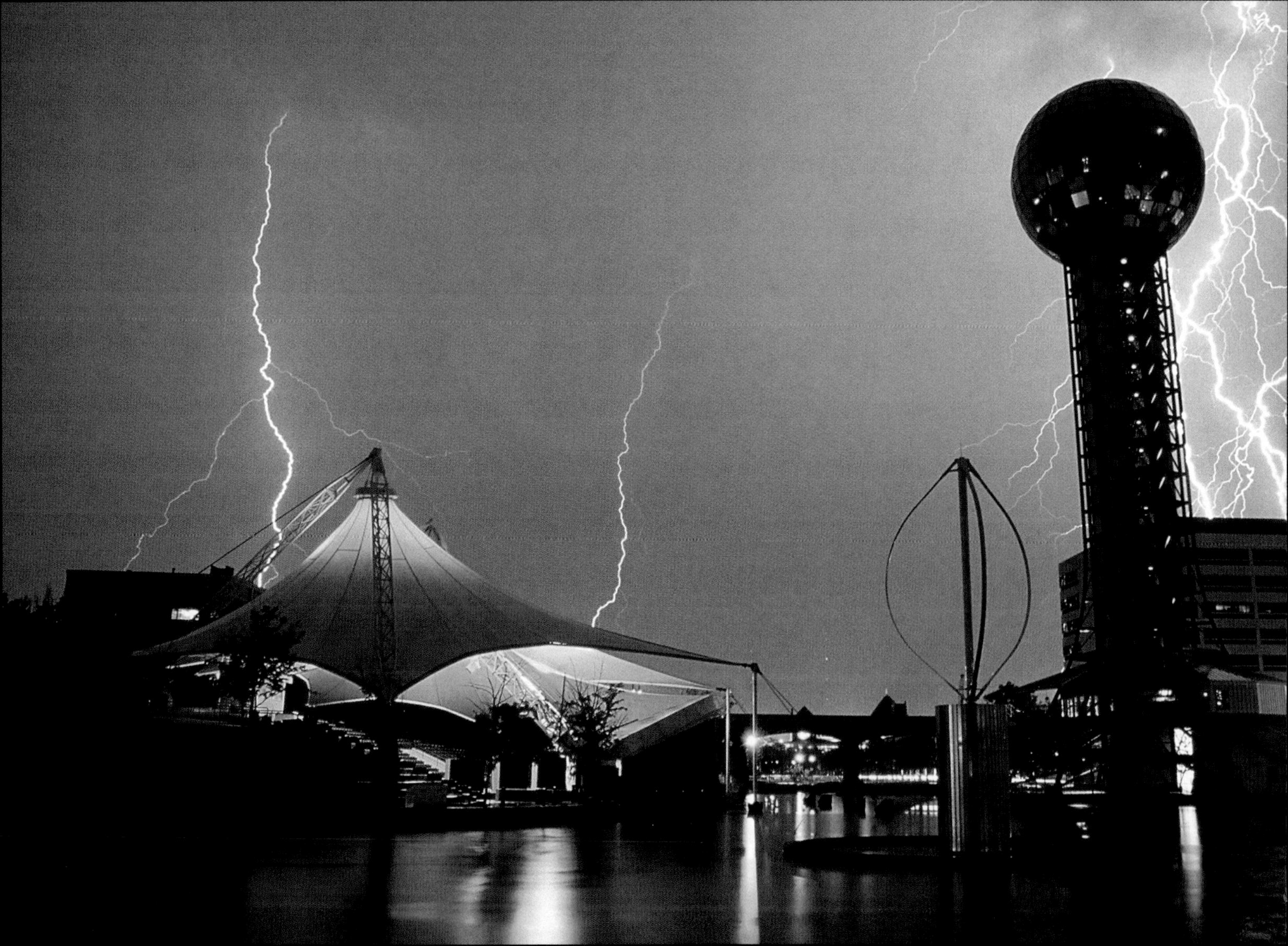

MOTHER NATURE LIGHTS up the night over two of Knoxville's most recog-

KNOXVILLE'S VARIED ARchitecture reflects the city's rich history in every medium, from simple brick to soaring glass.

Smoky Mountain Majesty

THROUGH THE LOOKING
glass: No matter how you
view it, the ongoing revital-
ization of downtown Knoxville gives
residents and visitors alike a fresh

CELEBRATORY FIREWORKS spotlight the 266-foot-tall Sunsphere, originally built downtown for the 1982 World's Fair. But the sparks really fly in Knoxville's business community. An average of $500 million annually is invested in the local economy for new companies and expansions.

Knoxville

Smoky Mountain Majesty

Knoxville

A MANTLE OF MIST SHROUDS Knoxville's Henley Street Bridge and the Riverwalk in somber reflection, belying the hubbub of activity the landmarks typically see every day.

EVEN THE SUNSPHERE'S bronze-coated glass windows echo the orange glow cast over the city by the University of Tennessee-Knoxville's Volunteer football team. Basking in the Vols' athletic successes, Dr. J. Wade Gilley (OPPOSITE BOTTOM), the university's 20th president, is equally determined to raise UT into the ranks of the nation's top 25 research universities.

OLUNTEER SPIRIT IS written all over the faces of Tennessee's legions of fans (PAGES 38-41). The university's marching band, Pride of the South-land (OPPOSITE CENTER), keeps spectators on their feet during halftime festivities, while Smokey, the bluetick coonhound who serves as the team's mascot, is always on his guard over Neyland Stadium during games.

Smoky Mountain Majesty

SCIENCE AND TECHNOLOGY have taken center stage in Knoxville's development.

with a fiber-optic network threading through the downtown area—the city bills itself as the place where

BERNADETTE AND SCOTT WEST ©

TRANSPORTATION IN Knoxville runs the gamut: Drivers have access to three interstate highways, and the airports, as well as the public Knoxville Area Transit (KAT) bus system, which conveys more than 2 million passengers to their destinations

46   Knoxville

WITH INTRICATE SILK patterns or durable panels of color, humans and arachnids weave their brilliant webs over Knoxville.

HETHER COATED WITH ice or cloaked in color, the natural beauty of Knoxville's landscape yields breathtaking vistas year-round.

AUNA AND FLORA THRIVE in Knoxville: Charming, affordable neighborhoods; more than 5,200 acres of park and recreation space; and proximity to Great Smoky Mountains National Park all render the city a highly attractive place to live (PAGES 52-55).

Knoxville

Smoky Mountain Majesty

KNOXVILLE'S TENNESSEE Theatre, originally opened on October 1, 1928, has been managed since 1997 by A.C. Entertainment, a local production and promotion company founded by Ashley Capps (OPPOSITE) and Troy Sellers. Among its many attributes, the Spanish-Moorish movie palace is home to a custom-built Mighty Wurlitzer pipe organ, nicknamed the Golden Voiced Wurlitzer, an attraction that still draws music fans today.

Knoxville

Knoxville

O NLY A HANDFUL OF people can lay claim to shaping a city, and Mark M. Schimmenti is one of them. An associate professor at the University of Tennessee's College of Architecture and Design, he has worked on urban design projects for firms from Miami to New York and Philadelphia, and he has left his mark on Knoxville as a consultant both to the city and to the East Tennessee Community Design Center.

Knoxville

ATER, WATER EVERY-
where? Located along the
Tennessee River, Knoxville
offers the opportunity for a plethora
of water-related activities. Some folks,
however, prefer to sharpen their skills
on terra firma before diving in.

WHETHER FISHING FOR food or for fun, sportsmen of all ages can take advantage of East Tennessee's watery resources, including some 300 miles of streams—containing more than 70 species of fish—at Great Smoky Mountains National Park. Enjoying the peace and quiet of the area's scenic beauty certainly helps to keep life in perspective (PAGES 64 AND 65).

Smoky Mountain Majesty

HOPING TO CATCH A glimpse of white-tailed deer or black bears, an estimated 2 million visitors per year drive Cades Cove's 11-mile sight-seeing loop road in Great Smoky Mountains National Park. For the more athletically inclined, the Big South Fork River and Recreation Area offers an array of mountainous hiking trails, including the path that climbs to the breathtaking spectacle of Angel Falls Overlook (OPPOSITE).

Hello, welcome to the Fruit & Berry Patch. Peaches are located straight back behind this barn about 300 yds. (Do not turn right at top of hill.) White peaches have an orange ribbon, yellow have a pink ribbon. Blueberries are immediately behind barn on right. Grapes are behind barn at the top of hill on right. Go out rear of barn, turn right and go about 150 yds for Blackberries. If no one is present, you may pick on the "Honor System". See instructions beside cash register. Thanks, Dennis Fox

SUNRISE, SUNSET: KNOX-villians who will settle for nothing less than the sun and the moon may find them well within reach—and ripe for the picking.

1786
JAMES WHITE'S FORT
205 E. HILL AVE.
OPEN   ADMITTANCE
MON. thru SAT.
9:30 - 4:30
LAST TOUR 3:30
CLOSED SUNDAY

MARK TWAIN
FAMILY
CABIN

HISTORY LIVES ON IN Knoxville, as evidenced by such attractions as James White's Fort (OPPOSITE), a reconstruction of the 1786 facility that was the first permanent pioneer structure built in the area. At John Rice Irwin's Museum of Appalachia, visitors can tour a number of buildings that have been relocated and restored. Among them is the Mark Twain Family Cabin (ABOVE), which was transported from Possum Trot, Tennessee, and which once housed part of Samuel Clemens' family—but not Twain himself. The legendary writer was born five months after his parents moved to Missouri.

Knoxville

ONCE THE HOME OF William Blount—governor of the territories south of the Ohio River from 1790 to 1796— Blount Mansion was built between 1792 and 1830. Today, visitors to the Knoxville-area attraction can travel back in time, viewing its authentic 18th-century furnishings and on-site exhibits.

Smoky Mountain Majesty

Saint John's Cathedral

SUMMER SERVICE
SCHEDULE
SUNDAYS
HOLY COMMUNION
CHORAL EUCHARIST
8:00 A.M.
10:00 A.M.
WEEKD

THE ROUGH STONEWORK and pointed-arch windows of Saint John's Cathedral, completed in 1892, tell the story of the church's seminal role in East Tennessee's religious development. In May 1844, its Episcopal congregation of 25 communicants became the first in the area to be admitted to the Tennessee Diocese.

AMONUMENT TO ENDURANCE, the Old Gray Cemetery marked its 150th anniversary in 2000, at which time it was also added to the National Register of Historic Places. The site's name is a tribute to 18th-century English poet Thomas Gray, who wrote "Elegy Written in a Country Church Yard."

As pastor of Mount Olive Baptist Church, Kelly M. Smith Jr. (RIGHT)—the son of a civil rights leader from Nashville—follows in his father's footsteps by serving as a strong role model for the members of his primarily African-American church. Ministering to their own flock, twins Helen L. Ashe and Ellen L. Turner (OPPOSITE, FROM LEFT) open up their Love Kitchen each Thursday to serve hot meals to more than 800 homeless, elderly, ill, and homebound patrons.

KNOXVILLE'S OPEN-DOOR friendliness is perhaps best exemplified by its hosting of not one, but two Ronald McDonald Houses. Home away from home for families of children undergoing cancer treatment, the nationwide low-cost housing centers first came to Tennessee via Knoxville in 1985. Exemplifying the centers' motto— The House that Love Built—the city opened its second site on Valentine's Day in February 2000.

Knoxville

T THE ENTRANCE TO THE Knoxville Museum of Art (OPPOSITE TOP), a replica of Robert Indiana's pop-art sculpture *Love* stands as a reminder that some emotions remain ageless.

THEIR PROCESS MIGHT BE low-tech, but the results are certainly cool. Co-owners Kevin Bradley (OPPOSITE) and Julie Belcher opened Yee-Haw Industrial Letterpress on Gay Street in 1999. To produce its distinctively funky prints, cards, fans, and other creations, the company employs the nearly extinct art of letterpress printing.

IN THE KNOXVILLE AREA, artistic expression knows few limits. World-renowned glass sculptor Richard Jolley (BOTTOM) is an Oak Ridge native whose delicate, colorful creations are on exhibit in countless museums and private collections. Stephen Wicks (TOP) indulges his own passion for art as curator of Collections and Exhibitions at the Knoxville Museum of Art. And Janice Forouzan (OPPOSITE), owner of downtown's Legacy Vintage Emporium, encourages her customers to transform themselves into works of art with mix-and-match fashions from bygone eras.

THE PAGEANTRY OF DRESSING up has become a living for two Knoxvillians. The winner of numerous contests and titles, Xena (ABOVE) owns a spot in the city's upper echelon of female imperson- ators. From classy second-hand items and antiques to full-fledged costumery, Ramona Didier (OPPOSITE) runs Big Don the Costumier—an offshoot of Big Don's Bargain Barn, started by her parents in 1952.

SHE GOT GAME: THE Women's Basketball Hall of Fame celebrated its grand opening in Knoxville in 1999, just two years after the hoopla of the WNBA's first season. The building's crowning glory—a 20,000-pound, steel-and-fiberglass basketball—was built by Minneapolis-based HSC Scenic Services, and is a to-scale replica of a regulation-sized basketball—right down to the 96,000 nubs on the ball's surface. Inside the hall, visitors are greeted by sculptor Elizabeth MacQueen's bronze statue, whose three figures represent the past, present, and future of women's basketball.

T'S HIGH ANXIETY EACH time Coach Pat Summit and her University of Tennessee-Knoxville Lady Volunteers take to the hardwood. Perennial NCAA tournament favorites, the Lady Vols had won six national titles as of the 2000 season. For her achievements, Summit was elected to the inaugural class of the Women's Basketball Hall of Fame in 1999, and, in 2000, became the fourth women's roundball coach to be selected for the Basketball Hall of Fame.

THEY ALL COULDA BEEN contenders: Nationally respected trainer and coach Ace Miller (OPPOSITE, ON LEFT) helped Jesse Byers (OPPOSITE, ON RIGHT) of Tellico Plains knock his way to the top as national welterweight champion. Any boxer worth his gloves, though, will tell you that there's a point at which it's best just to stay down on the mat.

ANY OF KNOXVILLE'S finest are women: In May 2000, the *Beloved Woman of Justice* sculpture (OPPOSITE), created by artist Audrey Flack, joined the police in upholding law and order outside the federal courthouse named for retired U.S. senator and former White House Chief of Staff Howard H. Baker Jr. The eagle and star atop the figure's headdress represent justice, righteousness, and integrity.

Smoky Mountain Majesty

101

FOR THOSE OF US WHO AREN'T fireproof, the Knoxville Fire Department—which boasts one of the South's most technologically advanced emergency fleets— answers in excess of 25,000 calls per year. Fire Captain Wm. Fred Baty (OPPOSITE) is also a certified wilderness paramedic, and he has developed and taught a number of courses, including three in wilderness medicine, at Roane State Community College.

BUILT IN 1886 AND PLACED on the National Register of Historic Places in 1973, the Knox County Courthouse (OPPOSITE) remains active today as a hub of government activity. The county's old courthouse (TOP), scene of many historic moments, now exists only as a photographic memory.

IE 92

OLD
KNOX COUNTY COURTHOUSE

The third courthouse of Knox County was across Main Ave. to the north from 1842-1886. There twelve Union raiders who were charged with train stealing in the 1862 Great Locomotive Chase in Georgia, were tried in 1863. One was convicted. The trial was then adjourned and the prisoners were sent to Atlanta because of increasing Union raids in East Tennessee. The courthouse was used as a hospital for the wounded of both armies in the fall of 1863.

TENNESSEE HISTORICAL COMMISSION

THEY LOVE THEIR JOBS: Hallerin Hilton Hill (LEFT), the long-reigning host of WNOX's popular *Hallerin Hill Morning Show*, has been named Best Talk Show Host five times by *Metro Pulse*, and his first book, *The Seven Pillars of Wisdom*, was released in 2000. First elected in 1987, Knoxville Mayor Victor Ashe (OPPOSITE) began his political career in the Tennessee House of Representatives in 1968. He is currently serving his fourth consecutive term at the city's helm.

Knoxville

DANCING TO THE TUNE of the inner child: Tony Lawson (TOP) hosts the weekday *Blue Plate Special* for the eclectic WDVX. Broadcasting from a 14-foot camper at the Fox Inn Campground in Clinton, Tennessee, the station plays everything from western swing to bluegrass and mountain music. At the popular Underground dance club, mix master DJ Storm (OPPOSITE TOP) spins records for his die-hard devotees.

© JONATHAN POSTAL / TOWERY PUBLISHING, INC.

STRINGS RULE: THE GUITAR remains a staple in Knoxville's music scene, whether it's being employed in the bluegrass tunes of acclaimed native son R.B. Morris (TOP) or Robinella and the CC String Band (OPPOSITE), or in Nocturna's (BOTTOM) self-described Southern-fried thrash metal.

KNOXVILLE PROVIDES A menu to suit every taste. Under the direction of co-owner Mahasti Vafaie (TOP), the Tomato Head on Market Square creates flavorful fare with ingredients such as goat cheese and pesto. South Knoxville's King Tut grill, owned and operated by the Girgis family (BOTTOM), serves authentic Egyptian cuisine, including a number of vegetarian dishes. In a more formal atmosphere, The Orangery's owner and executive chef David Pinckney (OPPOSITE) prepares fine continental cuisine for his diners. Pinckney has also donated his time and talents to the March of Dimes' Star Chefs Gourmet Auction.

Smoky Mountain Majesty

PRESERVING HISTORY IS A noble occupation, and one that inspires a number of Knoxville notables. Roy Garrett (OPPOSITE, TOP RIGHT) owns and operates Roy's Record Shop, piled high with vinyl 45s, while pianist/composer Donald Brown (OPPOSITE, TOP LEFT) has been instrumental in helping to revitalize Knoxville's jazz scene. The Blount Mansion Association (OPPOSITE BOTTOM) owns and preserves the historic 1792 structure, and operates tours of the premises. John Rice Irwin's Museum of Appalachia (RIGHT AND PAGES 116 AND 117) endeavors to keep the region's past alive through a number of events, including its annual Fall Homecoming, which combines traditional music and costuming with some startlingly modern accoutrements.

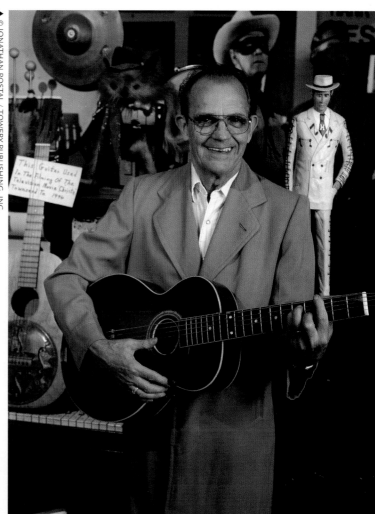

Knoxville

Smoky Mountain Majesty

WILD WILD WEST: "Marshal" Andy Smalls (LEFT) hosts Knoxville's *Riders of the Silver Screen*, a television show that debuted in 1990. Featuring classic Westerns and interviews with celebrities, the program also treats its audience to performances by Smalls and his Riders of the Silver Screen Band. For more than 45 years, Walter McGinnis (OPPOSITE), owner of Tri-City Barber Shop, has watched the area known as Old City evolve—from a warehouse district best known for brothels and street fights into a popular area for residents and sightseers.

BERNADETTE AND SCOTT WEST

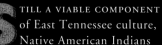

STILL A VIABLE COMPONENT
of East Tennessee culture,
Native American Indians

Knoxville

WHO'S WATCHING WHOM? A trip to the Knoxville Zoo, open year-round, promises hours of family fun. In addition to its white rhinoceroses, zebras, and African elephants, the zoo features a children's area where visitors can pet, brush, and feed llamas and other zoo inhabitants.

Smoky Mountain Majesty

THE INHERENT BEAUTY of birds spurs some to flights of fancy. As founder, president, and CEO of the Pigeon Forge-based American Eagle Foundation, Al Louis Cecere (ABOVE) focuses his eagle eye on developing bald-eagle protection programs, such as the one that saved Challenger (ABOVE), a permanently disabled—and therefore nonreleasable—bird. Ijams Nature Center's mascot, Environmental Man (OPPOSITE), uses costumes and creativity to make environmental education fun.

Knoxville

ake that! A miniature-golf club affords a pint-sized Knoxvillian plenty of protection against the formidable Tyrannosaurus Rex, helping maintain a sense of perspective when the world looms large.

ARVING OUT A NICHE IN East Tennessee's art community, Gary Ashton (RIGHT) of Mountain Spirits uses a chain saw to fashion his wooden creations. Knoxville potter Hugh Bailey (OPPOSITE) has made a specialty of his whimsical, wheel-thrown clay animals.

A S MUSIC DIRECTOR AND conductor of the Knoxville Symphony Orchestra—the Southeast's oldest continuing orchestra—Kirk Trevor (OPPOSITE, ON RIGHT) places an emphasis on working with other arts groups in the city, including the Knoxville Choral Society. Some locals, however, prefer a solo spotlight and a more secluded stage.

Knoxville

Some Knoxvillians wear their love for dancing as a badge of honor. Among the area's many dance organizations are the City Ballet of Knoxville and the Appalachian Ballet Company, which stages such annual favorites as *The Nutcracker*.

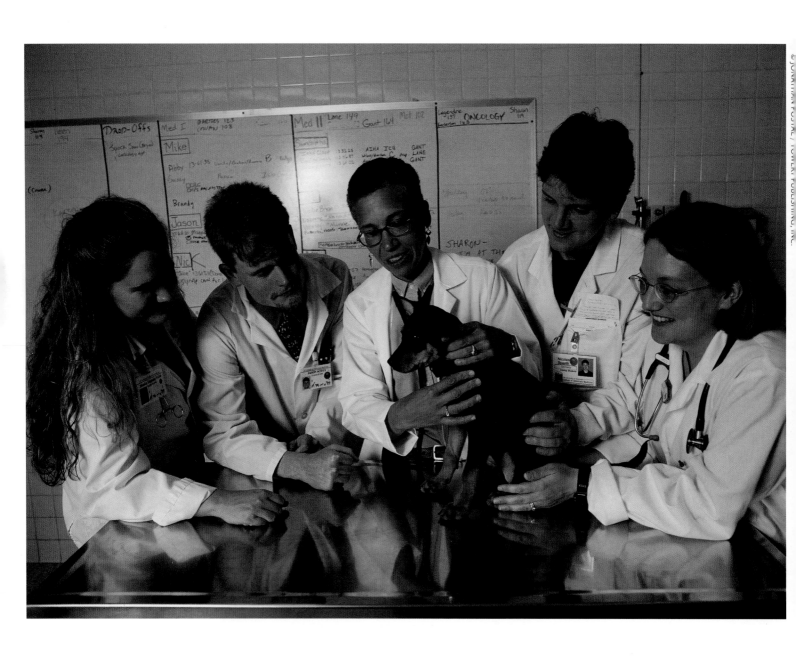

25 MARINE WAR DOGS GAVE THEIR LIVES LIBERATING
GUAM IN 1944. THEY SERVED AS SENTRIES, MESSENGERS, SCOUTS.
THEY EXPLORED CAVES, DETECTED MINES AND BOOBY TRAPS.
SEMPER FIDELIS

KURT	YONNIE	KOKO	BUNKIE
SKIPPER	PONCHO	TUBBY	HOBO
NIG	PRINCE	FRITZ	EMMY
MISSY	CAPPY	DUKE	MAX
BLITZ	ARNO	SILVER	BROCKIE
BURSCH	PEPPER	LUDWIG	RICKEY

TAM (BURIED AT SEA OFF ASAN POINT)
GIVEN IN THEIR MEMORY AND ON BEHALF OF THE SURVIVING MEN
OF THE 2nd AND 3rd MARINE WAR DOG PLATOONS, MANY OF WHOM
OWE THEIR LIVES TO THE BRAVERY AND SACRIFICE OF THESE
GALLANT ANIMALS
BY WILLIAM W. PUTNEY DVM C.O. 3rd DOG PLATOON
DEDICATED THIS DAY 21 JULY 1994

IN JULY 1998, A CEREMONY at the University of Tennessee unveiled a memorial (ABOVE) to 25 U.S. Marine war dogs—primarily Doberman pinschers—who were killed while serving alongside their human compatriots on Guam in 1944. Across campus, a dogged pursuit of excellence drives Dr. Tammy Anderson (OPPOSITE CENTER), an assistant professor at the university's College of Veterinary Medicine, as she guides her fourth-year students through the school's rigorous programs.

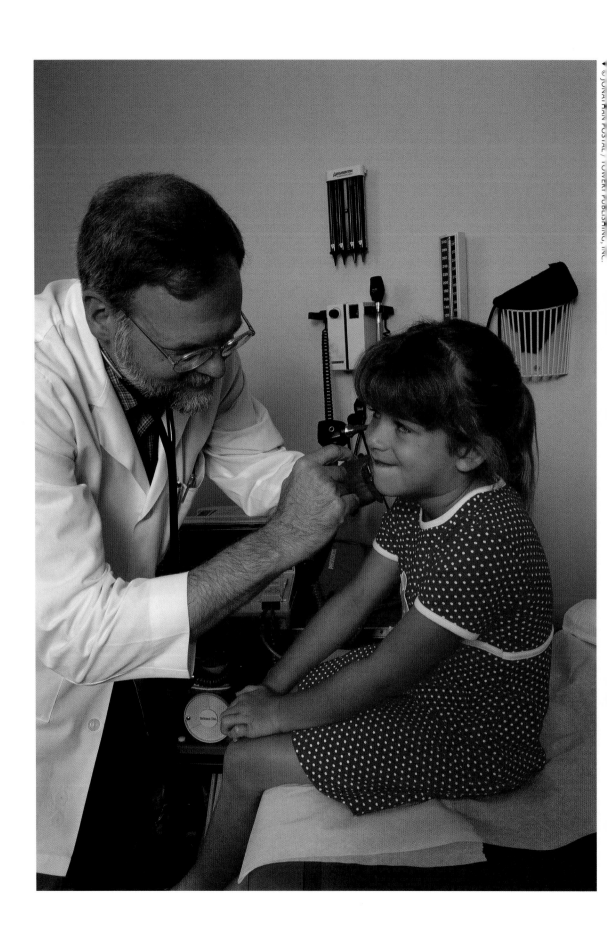

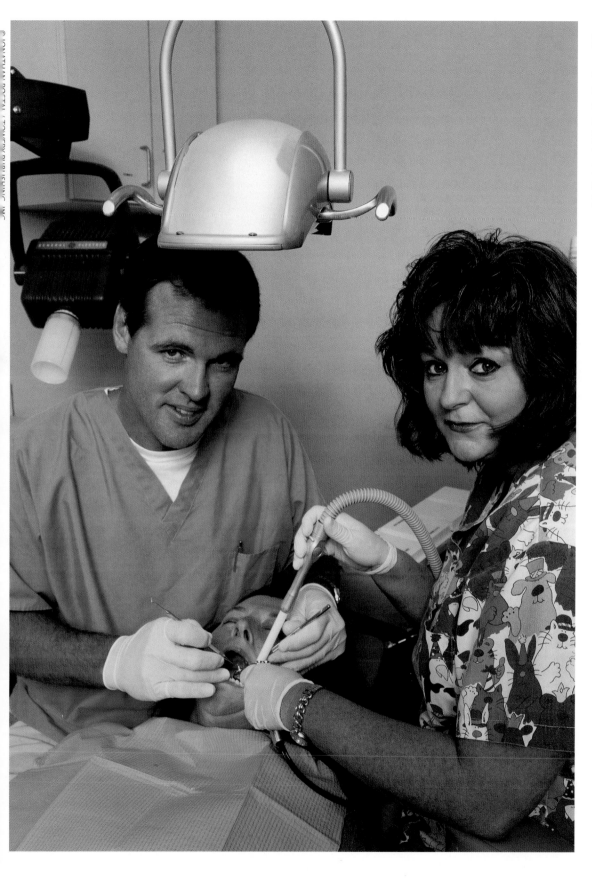

RIGINALLY OPENED in 1991, the nonprofit InterFaith Health Clinic exists to meet the primary health care needs of Knoxville's working uninsured and their families. Volunteering his dental skills to the clinic, Dr. Mark Evans joins forces with Vicki Monroe, RDA (LEFT) and Dr. Robert E. McDonald Jr. (OPPOSITE), medical director of the clinic, to help keep Knoxvillians healthy.

YOU'VE GOT TO HAND it to Knoxville's teachers: Engaging the minds of her sixth-grade students, Patricia Fitchpatrick (OPPOSITE) teaches science at Gresham Middle School, one of Knox County's 14 middle schools. In all, the county operates some 84 public schools, with an enrollment exceeding 51,000.

BOTH AUTHOR AND ILLUS-trator, Lisa Horstman (ABOVE) has drawn acclaim for her children's books. Her first— *Fast Friends*—garnered the Dr. Seuss Picture Book Award in 1994.

Keeping the literary bug alive, Karen Wilson (OPPOSITE, IN CAP), of the Pigeon Forge-based Dollywood Foundation's Imagination Library, reads to children aboard the Imagination Express. The library,

which currently provides a monthly book to every preschool child in Sevier County, plans to extend its reach across the country.

Knoxville

EAUTY, AS THEY SAY, IS
in the eye of the beholder,
and the city of Knoxville—
nestled in the majestic Smoky
Mountains— certainly offers plenty
to behold (PAGES 142-145).

Smoky Mountain Majesty

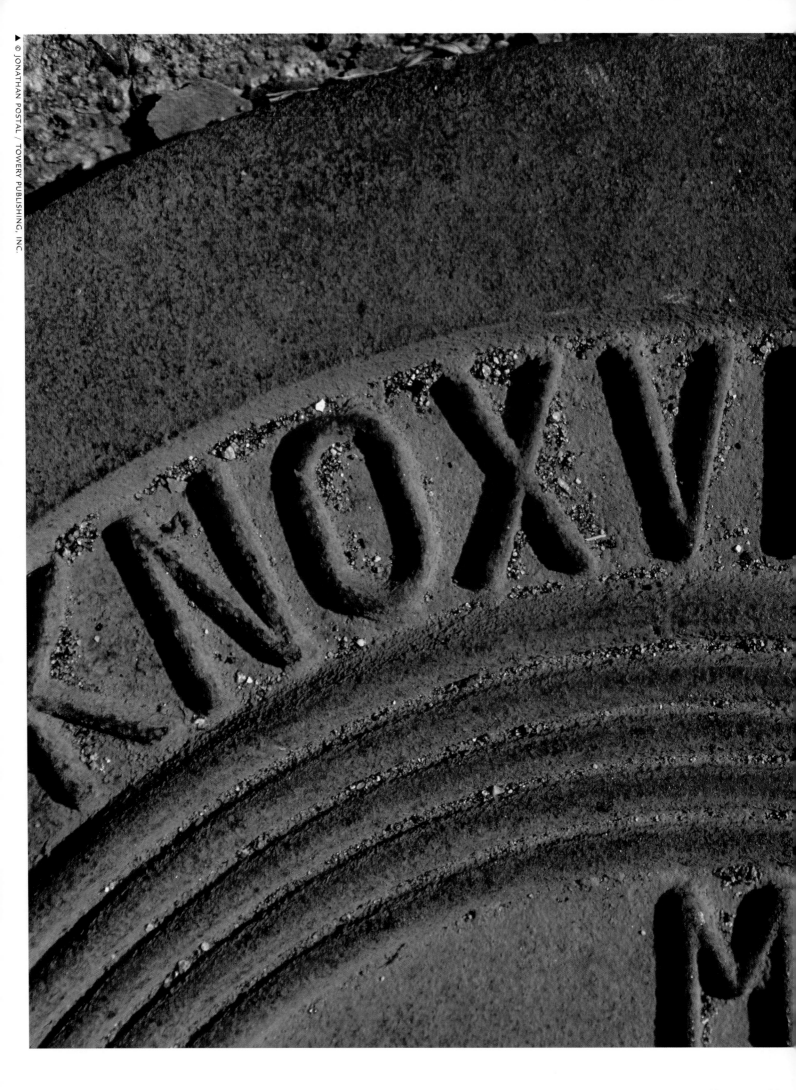

PROFILES IN EXCELLENCE

A look at the corporations, businesses, professional groups, and community service organizations that have made this book possible. Their stories—offering an informal chronicle of the local business community—are arranged according to the date they were established in Knoxville.

Alcoa Inc.
AmeriSteel
Arnett, Draper and Hagood
Bandit Lites, Inc.
Baptist Health System
Blount Memorial Occupational Health
Campbell, Cunningham & Taylor, P.C.
Cherokee Distributing Company
Community Reuse Organization of East Tennessee
Corporate Interiors
Covenant Health
Denark Construction, Inc.
Engert Plumbing and Heating, Inc.
Gulf & Ohio Railways
Hilton Knoxville
Home & Garden Television
Hyatt Regency Knoxville
Johnson & Galyon, Inc.
Kimberly-Clark Corporation
Knoxville Area Chamber Partnership
Knoxville Convention and Visitors Bureau
The Knoxville News-Sentinel
Knoxville Utilities Board
Marketing Dimensions
Martin & Company Investment Counsel
Matsushita Electronic Components Corporation
   of America
National Bank of Commerce
Parkway Realty Services/First Tennessee Plaza
Pellissippi State Technical Community College
Philips Consumer Electronics
Rice Automotive Group
St. Mary's Health System
Tennessee Valley Authority
Tindell's, Inc.
The Transition Team
The Trust Company of Knoxville
The University of Tennessee Medical Center
WATE-TV
Willis of Tennessee, Inc.
Zellweger Uster, Inc.

1868-1949

1868
AmeriSteel

1886
The Knoxville News-Sentinel

1891
Engert Plumbing and Heating, Inc.

1892
Tindell's, Inc.

1897
Willis of Tennessee, Inc.

1910
Alcoa Inc.

1914
Johnson & Galyon, Inc.

1920
Covenant Health

1930
St. Mary's Health System

1933
Tennessee Valley Authority

1939
Knoxville Utilities Board

1947
Blount Memorial Occupational Health

1948
Baptist Health System

1948
Zellweger Uster, Inc.

1949
Campbell, Cunningham & Taylor, P.C.

AmeriSteel

FROM MANUFACTURING CANNONBALLS DURING THE CIVIL WAR TO BECOMING PART OF ONE OF THE NATION'S LARGEST SUPPLIERS OF STEEL FOR CONCRETE-REINFORCING STEEL BARS (REBAR), AMERISTEEL'S KNOXVILLE STEEL MILL HAS FLOURISHED FOR MORE THAN 130 YEARS. LOCATED WEST OF DOWNTOWN KNOXVILLE, TUCKED ALONG THE EDGE OF THE LONSDALE COMMUNITY, THE COMPANY EMPLOYS SOME 300 MEN AND WOMEN.

AT AMERISTEEL, STEEL IS CONTINUOUSLY CAST INTO SQUARE SECTIONS KNOWN AS BILLETS, WHICH ARE CUT TO LENGTH AND STORED IN THE MILL'S BILLET YARD.

DURING THE STEELMAKING PROCESS, AMERISTEEL MELTS STEEL SCRAP IN AN ELECTRIC ARC FURNACE AT 3,000 DEGREES FAHRENHEIT.

AmeriSteel occupies a 40-acre site that serves as home for two major facilities: a steel mill that recycles 1,500 tons of scrap each day and a reinforcing steel plant that supplies fabricated reinforcing steel for major construction projects. Locally, AmeriSteel rebar can be found in such projects as the Tennessee Titans' new stadium, the Cumberland Gap tunnel, and Knoxville's Buck Karns Bridge. Projects outside the region include Chicago's Comiskey Park, the Pittsburgh airport, and Boston's Central Artery/Harbor Tunnel.

AmeriSteel's Knoxville Steel Mill was incorporated as the Knoxville Iron Company in 1868 and was located on the site of the foundry in the World's Fair Park. In 1902, the company moved to its present location on Tennessee Avenue in Lonsdale. Through the years, ownership of the mill has changed several times, but the facility has remained in constant

operation since its inception.

Initially, the mill refined pig iron into rolled wrought iron. In 1908, the mill began melting scrap iron and steel, and rolling the material into bars and other useful shapes at the rate of about 12,000 tons per year. In the 1940s, Ivan Racheff, a metallurgical consultant, began working

at the mill and began buying stock in the company. Racheff eventually owned 85 percent of the stock, and the mill grew under his leadership.

In 1957, three Vanderbilt University engineering graduates started Steel Service Company, a rebar fabricating company, in Nashville. In 1959, they opened a fabricating plant in Knoxville, and in 1968, they purchased the Knoxville Iron Company, one of their steel suppliers.

In 1974, Steel Service Company was purchased by Consolidated Gold Fields, a British company primarily involved in gold mining in South Africa. In 1987, Knoxville Iron Company and Steel Service Company were purchased by Tampa-based Florida Steel Corporation. And in 1994, Florida Steel Corporation became AmeriSteel.

AmeriSteel, a subsidiary of Brazilian-based steelmaker Gerdau, S.A., operates electric furnace steel minimills in Charlotte; Jacksonville, Florida; and Jackson and Knoxville, Tennessee, with a combined capacity of about 2 million tons of raw steel per year. In addition, the company operates 18 downstream rebar fabricating plants along the East Coast and west to Memphis. AmeriSteel also operates a collated nail and wire mesh fabricating facility in New Orleans, and a railroad track spike manufacturing operation with plants

in Lancaster, South Carolina, and
Paragould, Arkansas.

The Manufacturing Process

AmeriSteel manufactures all
of its steel from recycled steel
scrap. With its two mills in Tennessee,
AmeriSteel is the largest recycler in the
state. Every day the Knoxville Steel
Mill alone recycles the equivalent of
1,000 junked automobiles into useful
steel products. In 2000, a new, $35
million melt shop was placed into
service at the Knoxville mill, increasing the facility's output by 15 percent
to 450,000 tons of steel per year.

During the steelmaking process,
steel scrap is melted in an electric arc
furnace at 3,000 degrees Fahrenheit.
The molten steel is analyzed, and
various alloys are added to maximize
its strength. The steel is then poured
into a ladle and taken to the casting
machine. There, the steel is continuously cast into square sections known
as billets. The billets are cut to length
and stored in the billet yard.

From the billet yard, the billets
are taken by overhead crane to the
rolling mill, where they are heated
in a reheat furnace to 2,200 degrees.
They are then passed through a series
of pinch rollers known as stands.
Here, the steel billet is rolled into
its eventual size and shape, and cut
into lengths according to customer
requirements. The finished steel is
then warehoused or shipped to an

AmeriSteel customer, to one of
AmeriSteel's own fabricating shops,
or to an independent fabricator or
steel service center.

Knoxville is the only city where
AmeriSteel operates a steel mill, a
rebar fabricating plant, and an epoxy-
coating fabricating plant all on the
same site. Epoxy coating adds cor-
rosion resistance to the rebar.

Strong Community Ties

Recent decisions to expand operations in Knoxville, typified
by the new melt shop, are a direct
indication of AmeriSteel's confidence
in the city's business climate. According to a statement from AmeriSteel
officials: "Knoxville has proven it is
interested in helping industry grow.
The city, the Mayor, the Chamber
Partnership, the Development Corporation, and the State of Tennessee
all deserve credit for creating an
atmosphere where we felt welcome."

The company enjoys a rich and
rewarding history of strong ties to
the community. Racheff strongly
believed that steel and nature could
exist side by side, and in the 1940s,
he built one of Knoxville's most attractive public gardens next door to
the mill. Today, the house that served
as the original office and the gardens
attract visitors from all over the region,
particularly during the Dogwood
Arts Festival. The company assists
the Tennessee Federated Garden Club
in maintaining this local treasure.

As rebar plays an integral role
in strengthening the concrete in
America's buildings, so too does
AmeriSteel play an integral role in
helping to strengthen the Knoxville
community. With an ongoing commitment to producing top quality
products in state-of-the-art facilities,
AmeriSteel will continue to be an
active participant on the Knoxville
business scene well into the future.

AMERISTEEL IS ONE OF THE NATION'S
LARGEST SUPPLIERS OF STEEL FOR
CONCRETE-REINFORCING STEEL BARS
(REBAR).

AMERISTEEL OCCUPIES A 40-ACRE SITE
THAT SERVES AS HOME FOR TWO MAJOR
FACILITIES: A STEEL MILL THAT RECYCLES
1,500 TONS OF SCRAP EACH DAY AND A
REINFORCING STEEL PLANT THAT SUPPLIES
FABRICATED REINFORCING STEEL FOR
MAJOR CONSTRUCTION PROJECTS.

The Knoxville News-Sentinel

YEAR AFTER YEAR, THE KNOXVILLE NEWS-SENTINEL IS RECOGNIZED FOR QUALITY JOURNALISM. AFTER WAGING A TWO-YEAR BATTLE TO OBTAIN ACCESS TO PUBLIC RECORDS ON COURT PROCEEDINGS, THE NEWS-SENTINEL RECEIVED THE SCRIPPS HOWARD FOUNDATION AWARD FOR DISTINGUISHED SERVICE TO THE FIRST AMENDMENT AND THE ASSOCIATED PRESS MANAGING EDITORS FREEDOM OF INFORMATION AWARD. THE

newspaper has also received the Enterprise Foundation/Freedom Forum's Excellence in Urban Journalism Award, and many state and regional awards.

While *The Knoxville News-Sentinel's* list of awards and accolades is a long one, Publisher Bruce Hartmann says they reflect what is most important to the communities the newspaper serves. "Our greatest accomplishments are the integrity of the editorial content we produce each day and the credibility of the news," Hartmann emphasizes.

Legacy as a Community Watchdog

The first *Knoxville Sentinel* was published in 1886 by John Travis Hearn on an old steam-operated, flatbed press. In 1921, Scripps McRae, later known as Scripps Howard, founded the *Knoxville News*; in 1926, Scripps Howard bought the *Sentinel* and merged the two papers.

The newspaper moved into its downtown Knoxville location in 1928. The facilities would expand to serve its needs for nearly 80 years. In 1975, computers replaced typewriters; in 1986, the newspaper converted from an afternoon to a morning paper. Later technology advances improved the quality of the newspaper.

Today, *The Knoxville News-Sentinel* has a weekday circulation of about 125,000 and a Sunday circulation of some 162,000. Special sections offer local news in Blount County, Anderson County, North Knoxville, and West Knoxville.

Harry Moskos, longtime editor, notes that the paper undergoes constant improvement to ensure it reflects the interests of the Knoxville metropolitan area. For example, Moskos notes that the business section runs daily with a variety of regular themes, including personal finance on Monday, construction and real estate on Wednesday, technology on Thursday, and weekend stocks on Saturday. A

travel section has been added on Sunday, and the daily feature sections have also expanded with themes, such as health, fitness, and science on Monday; food on Wednesday; fashion on Thursday; home and garden on Friday; and family and religion on Saturday.

Moskos says that he views the newspaper as "the conscience of the community," and that his objective always has been to provide accurate and fair reporting, along with easy access for the community. "Our goal is to put out a product that is interesting and of service to readers in East Tennessee, to be in sync with the community," Moskos explains.

Media Expansion to Meet Future Needs

Technology and the World Wide Web are increasingly becoming an integral part of communications in the 21st century, and that is certainly true at *The News-Sentinel*. "The Knoxville News-

THE KNOXVILLE NEWS-SENTINEL'S NATIONALLY RECOGNIZED EDUCATION PROGRAM ASSISTS TEACHERS AND STUDENTS IN 20 EAST TENNESSEE COUNTIES. THIS SUPPORT PROGRAM HELPS TO IMPROVE READING AND MATH SKILLS, AS WELL AS CREATING STUDENT AWARENESS OF THEIR COMMUNITIES.

Sentinel sponsors more than 250 community and educational programs each year.

The News-Sentinel Expo 10,000 is the largest road race in the East Tennessee area. The Women Today Expo reaches thousands of women with hundreds of exhibitors. *The News-Sentinel* in Education and its literacy programs have won five national awards and touched some 58,000 schoolchildren in Knox County alone. *The News-Sentinel* also serves the community through charity programs including the Empty Stocking, Milk, and Mercy funds.

Investment in Downtown

In May 2000, *The Knoxville News-Sentinel* announced plans to move its headquarters to a new, $45 million facility just two miles from its Church Avenue location. With the move, the newspaper will become the anchor tenant in a 90-acre redevelopment tract known as the Center City Business Neighborhood.

With a planned move at the end of 2002, Hartmann says the new office and production facilities will provide *The News-Sentinel* one of the most automated production environments in the industry, with faster presses, better packaging, and increased color capacity. In addition, the new facilities will enable later deadlines and earlier delivery times for the paper.

"Whether via paper, on-line, or the mail, *The Knoxville News-Sentinel* is the leading information provider in the market," Hartmann points out. "This new facility will allow us to continue in that role."

THE KNOXVILLE NEWS-SENTINEL'S 22ND ANNUAL EXPO 10,000 DREW MORE THAN 1,800 RUNNERS IN 5K AND 10K SPRING RACES FOR COMPETITIVE AND NONCOMPETITIVE RUNNERS OF ALL AGES.

Sentinel is in the business of information, and local news is our franchise," notes Hartmann.

The newspaper's main Web site is KnoxNews.com. Several Web sites have been developed to focus on local information niches: GoVols.com, GoLadyVols.com, and GoSmokies.com highlight local sports and the nearby Great Smoky Mountains. Newer sites include KnoxCars.com, *Home Market* magazine on-line, and KnoxCareers.com.

"There are so many sources of news and information in this information age," Hartmann acknowledges. "*The Knoxville News-Sentinel* has been here for more than 100 years, and we will always be here through print, Web sites, direct mail, E-mail, and other technologies that may develop. You can always count on us to provide information to our community."

Commitment to Community

Every year, the company supports numerous local, civic, charitable, and educational organizations. Direct donations total close to $500,000 annually, and in-kind donations contribute another $1 million or more to the community. In addition, *The Knoxville News-*

HUNDREDS OF EMPTY STOCKING FUND BOXES BRIMMING WITH PRODUCE AND GROCERIES COVER THE FLOOR OF THE JACOB BUILDING AT CHILHOWEE PARK. THE EMPTY STOCKING FUND ALSO PROVIDES TOYS AND BOOKS FOR CHILDREN IN MORE THAN 3,800 HOUSEHOLDS ANNUALLY.

Engert Plumbing and Heating, Inc.

ENGERT PLUMBING AND HEATING, INC. WAS FORMALLY ESTABLISHED IN KNOXVILLE IN 1891 BY NATIVE-BORN FREDERIC A. "FRITZ" ENGERT, THE SON OF GERMAN IMMIGRANTS. BY THE TIME HE WAS 17, HE WAS WORKING LOCALLY AS A PLUMBER, AND BY THE TIME HE WAS 21, HE WAS BUILDING A RESPECTED PLUMBING BUSINESS THAT SURVIVES TO THIS DAY. ENGERT PLUMBING AND HEATING HAS STAYED IN THE FAMILY FOR THREE

generations. James G. Johnston Jr., current president and general manager, is the nephew of Frank Engert, Fritz Engert's nephew.

The roots of Engert Plumbing and Heating are deep in East Tennessee. The staff and owners are constantly learning to improve their profession, and they have propelled the company into the position of having one of the most recognized names in the industry, successfully competing with new companies from around the country.

Knoxville's Landmarks

The Engert business is classified as a mechanical contracting business with specialties in plumbing, heating, and air-conditioning. In the early days, Engert worked with Miller's department store on Gay Street, which was the first air-conditioned department store in Knoxville. Engert also designed, manufactured, and installed aluminum ceiling panels in that store and later created an igloo setting where children could visit Santa Claus.

Other Knoxville landmarks that turned to Engert include the Pickle

and Turner Building in 1894; Knoxville Knitting Mills in 1895; the Arnstein Building, Knoxville's first skyscraper, in 1905; and the Bijou Theatre in 1909. Engert has worked on other major projects such as hospitals, churches, and the University of Tennessee (UT) Veterinary School, as well as the university's Communications Building, Admin-

istration Building, Gibbs Hall, and apartments for married students.

In Oak Ridge, Engert Plumbing worked on X-10, otherwise known as the Mouse House, which was the first experimental radiological laboratory to be built in the area. Also, all water meters for the City of Oak Ridge were installed by Engert. The company built and installed a huge oven at Rohm & Haas, as well as installing and maintaining the lines and depots for Southern Railroad. Other notable jobs include the Holiday Inn World's Fair; Riverview Towers; the Federal Courthouse, formerly the Whittle Building; and the Schlegel Mixing Plant. Engert was also involved in the renovation of the old Miller's Building.

"We work on a wide variety of jobs," says Johnston. "We have succeeded because so many of our customers are repeat customers. We can build and install whatever details and energy needs our customer wants."

Rich in History

The Engert offices are located in the McCammon Home. The home for Samuel McCammon was completed in 1854 on the site

ENGERT PLUMBING AND HEATING, INC. HAS BEEN A PART OF THE ENGERT FAMILY SINCE 1891. BEGUN BY FREDERIC A. "FRITZ" ENGERT (BOTTOM LEFT), THE COMPANY WAS RUN FROM 1935 TO 1974 BY FRANK ENGERT (BOTTOM RIGHT). TODAY, JAMES G. JOHNSTON JR. (TOP), FRANK'S NEPHEW, SERVES AS PRESIDENT AND GENERAL MANAGER.

willing to do first-class work. If you treat them fairly, they'll come back and perform fairly. That's the way it has been all through the Engert years, and it is our pledge as long as we are in business. We now continue well into our second century of service holding to the trust and dependability that architects, builders, and owners have identified with Engert Plumbing and Heating, Inc."

As Fritz Engert once said, "We continue to serve the customer as we would ourselves."

ENGERT PLUMBING AND HEATING OPERATES OUT OF THE HISTORIC MCCAMMON HOME (TOP RIGHT), RESTORED BY THE COMPANY IN 1955. ENGERT'S MARK CAN BE SEEN ALL OVER KNOXVILLE, FROM THE ARNSTEIN BUILDING (BOTTOM), CIRCA 1905—THE CITY'S FIRST SKYSCRAPER— TO THE MILLER'S BUILDING (TOP LEFT), THE FIRST EAST TENNESSEE FACILITY TO HAVE AIR-CONDITIONING.

of the James White home. Carefully restored by the Engerts in 1955, the McCammon Home is listed on the National Register of Historic Places and has been recognized with an award from Knoxville Heritage.

The two-story, 50-by-20-foot McCammon Home was built of handmade brick fired on the site. Engert has doubled its office space, taking care to protect the historic integrity of the original structure. The company's manufacturing shop now sits on the site of an old barn and work shed.

Stories and tales of ghosts have existed from the early days before Engert occupied the McCammon Home. Employees have reported hearing footsteps when the building was quiet. Speculation as to exactly where the sounds come from is as varied as the many who have heard them.

A Family Business That Has Survived

Johnston started working summer jobs at Engert at the age of 15. "When I was old enough to drive, I worked there delivering materials to the jobs," he recalls. "Then I

got into a little bit of plumbing and a little bit of pipe fitting." After graduating from UT, Johnston worked at Robert Shaw Controls before his uncle, Frank Engert, called and asked him to come back to the family business. Johnston became general manager of the company in 1965, and when the company was incorporated in 1973, he was named president.

The management and employees remember the generosity of Frank Engert, as well as his business acumen. They say he and his wife, Ellen, set high standards, which Johnston continues to follow today. Engert led the company through a period of intensive growth, from the postdepression years through the mid-sixties.

Today, Johnston notes that Engert continues to work on many projects for hospitals in the East Tennessee area. Handling their constantly changing mechanical requirements keeps the Engert staff of about 130 busily occupied.

"Anybody can buy pipe, and anybody can buy fittings, but what you need are the dedicated people to put it all together," Johnston says. "You need people who are dedicated and

Smoky Mountain Majesty

Tindell's, Inc.

MORE THAN 100 YEARS AGO, CARL TINDELL'S GRANDFATHER STARTED THE FAMILY BUSINESS WITH A STEAM-POWERED SAWMILL THAT HE TOOK FROM ONE TIMBER TRACT TO ANOTHER THROUGHOUT THE WOODS OF KNOX, UNION, AND ANDERSON COUNTIES. CARL FOLLOWED IN THE FOOTSTEPS OF HIS FATHER, FRANCIS TINDELL, AND HIS GRANDFATHER, FATE TINDELL, WHEN HE JOINED THE FAMILY BUSINESS IN 1964.

CLOCKWISE FROM TOP:
TINDELL'S, INC.'S COMMODITY CENTER, LOCATED AT THE FORKS OF THE RIVER INDUSTRIAL PARK, DISTRIBUTES BULK COMMERCIAL AND RESIDENTIAL ORDERS.

WHEN TINDELL'S BEGAN IN 1892, LEDGERS WERE USED TO TRACK BUSINESS.

TINDELL'S TRUSS PLANT PRODUCES ROOF TRUSSES, FLOOR TRUSSES, AND WALL PANELS FOR HOME BUILDERS AND INDUSTRIAL CONTRACTORS.

For the past four decades, he has led a company that evolves as its customers evolve.

Today, Tindell's, Inc. is recognized as one of the largest building materials suppliers in East Tennessee. The company recorded sales in excess of $31 million in 1999 and provided a healthy livelihood for 155 employees. Instead of a sawmill, the company has grown into a strong, business-to-business manufacturer and supplier of building materials.

"The highly energetic working atmosphere created by our well-trained and professional management staff encourages creativity, empowerment, and teamwork," explains Carl Tindell, president. "Our management team is guided by a shared strategic vision and inspired to be responsive to market requirements." As a result, Tindell's delivers superior service to its professional customers consistent

with its mission statement: "Tindell's mission is to provide consistently high quality products and service to our customers through innovation, efficiency, and integrity."

At the core of its business, the company manufactures, installs, and sells building materials to professional building contractors. Four sales facilities are strategically located in Knoxville, LaFollette, Oak Ridge, and Sevierville to serve its customers. The company's installed sales division provides value-added services through installation of garage doors, fireplaces, insulation, windows, doors, cabinets, mirrors, and shelving.

Tindell's operates two manufacturing facilities: a truss plant and a millwork division, both of which are located in Knoxville. The truss plant produces roof trusses, floor trusses, and wall panels for home builders and industrial contractors. The mill-

work division produces interior and exterior door units. A commodity center, located at the Forks of the River Industrial Park, distributes bulk commercial and residential orders.

Tindell's corporate office is located on Norris Freeway in Halls, where the staff provides management and administrative support for the sales and manufacturing divisions. The company is heavily dedicated to community service, including helping to build the gazebo for a new community park, as well as donating time and materials to the community's new Boys and Girls Clubs, Habitat for Humanity, and YMCA.

"At Tindell's, we have a commitment to processes that harness the power of bottom-up understanding of customers," Tindell says. "By focusing attention on a desired leadership position, measuring progress, and continually seeking new ways to serve customers better, the actions and aspirations of Tindell's are given new meaning. Tindell's management understands that there really is only one valid definition of our business purpose: to create a satisfied customer. As in the past, so in the future: it is the customer who determines what our business is and what it will be."

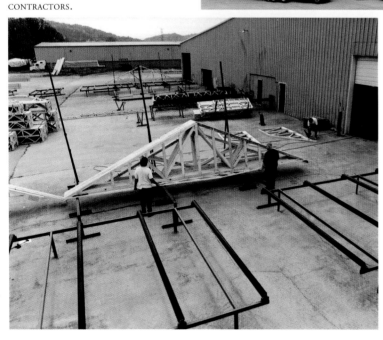

A FTER PROTECTING THE ASSETS OF INDIVIDUALS AND BUSINESSES IN EAST TENNESSEE FOR MORE THAN 100 YEARS, KNOXVILLE-BASED INSURANCE BROKER WILLIS OF TENNESSEE, INC. IS POISED FOR ANOTHER CENTURY OF GROWTH AND SERVICE TO THIS COMMUNITY. ■ "OUR FOUNDER, M.F. FLENNIKEN, ESTABLISHED A SOLID BASE FOR THIS COMPANY BY STAYING AHEAD OF THE CONSTANTLY

Willis of Tennessee, Inc.

changing business trends of our clients and their industries," says Joe Ben Turner, president and CEO of Willis of Knoxville. "We've worked diligently to follow in his footsteps, providing innovative risk management and insurance solutions to our clients' needs."

Created in Knoxville in 1897, the M.F. Flenniken Company prospered for 84 years before merging in 1981 with New York-headquartered Corroon & Black Corporation, one of the world's largest full-service insurance brokers. After nearly a decade, the firm expanded globally, merging with British-based Willis Faber, and in 1999, simply shortened its name to Willis.

Third Largest in the World

Today, Willis is the world's third-largest insurance brokerage firm with international headquarters in London and U.S. headquarters in Nashville. The company employs some 11,500 people, including some 65 in Knoxville, and has annual revenues of more than $1.3 billion.

Willis serves a broad spectrum of corporate and institutional clients. The insurance carriers that the firm represents enjoy the industry's top ratings from such companies as *Best's Key Rating Guide* and Standard and Poor's. The Travelers Insurance Company is one of these carriers and has been associated with Willis of Knoxville for more than 100 years.

Knoxville Office Accolades

Willis has earned the business of numerous small and large Knoxville-based companies," Turner points out. "Several of these have been clients of Willis and its predecessor companies for over 50 years."

The firm offers a variety of insurance products in its five divisions: commercial, construction, employee

benefits, environmental, and personal insurance. Willis, USA is recognized as the largest writer of environmental coverage in the United States, and Knoxville is one of the nation's leading producers of environmental business.

Every year, Willis recognizes its leading U.S. office for superior sales and customer satisfaction. The Knoxville office has won this distinction in eight of the 12 years since its inception—including 1996 through 2000.

Turner attributes this honor and other successes to the experienced staff of the Knoxville office. In addition to Turner, who joined the local office in 1968, the Knoxville office of Willis offers approximately 700 years of combined experience. Seven members of the team have been with the firm for more than 30 years, while another six have been with Willis more than 20 years.

Community Commitment

We're deeply proud of our city's rich heritage and are pleased to have played an important role in making Knoxville a great community," Turner notes. In addition to Turner's post as past chairman of the boards for the Greater Knoxville Chamber of Commerce, East Tennessee Heart Association,

and Westminster Presbyterian Church boards of trustees, many of Willis' other professionals exemplify the company's commitment to the community. Turner and other Willis professionals have served on many local boards, including United Way, Leadership Knoxville, Fort Sanders Foundation, Knoxville Museum of Art, St. Mary's Hospital, Knoxville Zoo, Dream Connection, Boys Club & Girls Club, Nucleus, Juvenile Diabetes Association, YWCA, Knox Area Rescue Ministries, and Alzheimer's Association.

"Our commitment to this community permeates throughout the Willis organization," Turner adds. "We know that, combined with serving more than 7,000 clients in East Tennessee, we're protecting our city's economy and investing in its future."

KNOXVILLE-BASED WILLIS OF TENNESSEE, INC. HAS BEEN A PROMINENT MEMBER OF THE CITY'S BUSINESS COMMUNITY SINCE 1897. GUIDING THE COMPANY INTO ITS SECOND CENTURY ARE (SEATED, FROM LEFT) RON ALEXANDER, EXECUTIVE VICE PRESIDENT AND COO; JOE BEN TURNER, PRESIDENT AND CEO; ROCKY GOODE, EXECUTIVE VICE PRESIDENT; WILLIAM HAMILTON, SENIOR VICE PRESIDENT; (STANDING, FROM LEFT) JOHN MILAM, SENIOR VICE PRESIDENT; AND WILLIAM GLENN, EXECUTIVE VICE PRESIDENT.

Alcoa Inc.

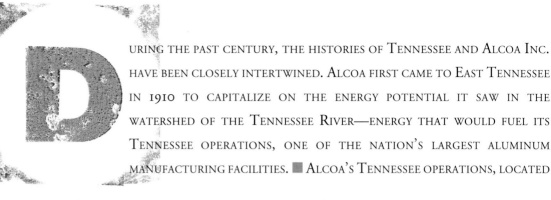

DURING THE PAST CENTURY, THE HISTORIES OF TENNESSEE AND ALCOA INC. HAVE BEEN CLOSELY INTERTWINED. ALCOA FIRST CAME TO EAST TENNESSEE IN 1910 TO CAPITALIZE ON THE ENERGY POTENTIAL IT SAW IN THE WATERSHED OF THE TENNESSEE RIVER—ENERGY THAT WOULD FUEL ITS TENNESSEE OPERATIONS, ONE OF THE NATION'S LARGEST ALUMINUM MANUFACTURING FACILITIES. ■ ALCOA'S TENNESSEE OPERATIONS, LOCATED

near the Knoxville airport in Blount County, makes basic aluminum and then fabricates the aluminum into sheet for aluminum cans. The large coils of aluminum sheet are shipped around the world and used to make aluminum beverage cans. Approximately 1,800 East Tennesseans work at the facility.

Some 10 years ago, Alcoa again looked to East Tennessee—this time as a potential new home for two of its largest business units, Alcoa Rigid Packaging and Alcoa Primary Metals. These businesses, formerly headquartered in Pittsburgh, relocated to downtown Knoxville in 1990 and, combined with Alcoa's Tennessee Operations, have forged a 100-year history in East Tennessee—a history of industry, progress, and community responsibility.

Located in the Riverview Tower, the downtown office houses an additional 200 employees and serves as global headquarters for the Alcoa Rigid Packaging business unit and U.S. headquarters for the Alcoa

Primary Metals business unit. Together, these businesses now account for approximately $6 billion of the company's total annual revenue. Knoxville also is home to Alcoa's global energy division and metal-purchasing activities.

Global Company

The company's Knoxville-based business units are only two of Alcoa's businesses located around the globe. The firm has operating locations in 36 countries and employs more than 140,000 people. Alcoa's customers represent the packaging, consumer, automotive, aerospace, and construction industries, among others.

"There is no doubt that the natural resources of East Tennessee are the main reasons that Alcoa came to this region in 1910 and again in 1990," says Mike Coleman, Alcoa corporate vice president and president of the Alcoa Rigid Packaging business unit. "While these resources undoubtedly included an abundance

of hydropower, which is critical to aluminum production, the most important resource this region provided was—and continues to be—its people.

"Throughout Alcoa's history in the Knoxville area, East Tennesseans have been critical to our success through their work ethic, their drive for success, and an undying commitment to this community," says Coleman. "These characteristics are also true of the hundreds of new Tennesseans who have been transplanted to this area as Alcoa employees over the years. All citizens of this region are the beneficiaries of the work these people have provided. Blount County and Knoxville Alcoans have provided this region with a stable, safe, and environmentally sound industry, plus a better place to live, thanks to the hours of community service they provide each year."

The Alcoa Rigid Packaging business unit has operating locations on four continents, and its aluminum

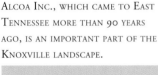

ALCOA INC., WHICH CAME TO EAST TENNESSEE MORE THAN 90 YEARS AGO, IS AN IMPORTANT PART OF THE KNOXVILLE LANDSCAPE.

sheet products are used exclusively to make aluminum cans for a variety of food and beverage products. The Alcoa Recycling Company, also a part of the Alcoa Rigid Packaging business unit, ensures that the vast majority of beverage containers sold are recycled into new cans, thus saving precious raw materials and energy.

Lloyd Jones, president of Alcoa's U.S. Smelting business unit and a native Australian, says the diversity of employees' backgrounds in his office greatly contributes to its success in the competitive international business climate. "We're fortunate to have employees from different continents and cultural origins," says Jones. "It offers the dynamic work environment necessary to conduct global business."

The Alcoa Primary Metals business unit is a network of domestic metal-producing plants, which crank out almost 2 million metric tons of aluminum per year. This metal is used by other Alcoa fabricating facilities and external customers producing a variety of aluminum products.

Community Minded

While Alcoa is focused on providing quality products, the company is also highly dedicated to supporting and maintaining a high quality of life in its community. Alcoa and its employees support the East Tennessee community through multiple Alcoa Foundation grants, seasonal community service projects, and annual employee charitable giving.

Coleman affirms that a strong emphasis is placed upon employee community service contributions. "Several times each year, employees team in various community service projects that benefit local charities," says Coleman. "How we spend our time off the job is discretionary; I'm very proud that our employees choose to spend some of it in community service. Whether it's helping to build a Habitat for Humanity home with funds raised from recycling aluminum cans, or participating in our annual volunteer day projects, Alcoa lends its support by continually giving back to our East Tennessee community—a place we've called home for a combined century."

Johnson & Galyon, Inc.

At Johnson & Galyon, Inc., a leading general contractor firm in the Knoxville area that is nearly a century old, the motto "taking dead aim" means targeting a task, completing it on schedule, and doing it well. Symbolized by the plumb bob hanging on a string, the phrase heralds the beginning of each new endeavor at the company—with challenges to maintain accuracy and perfection throughout the project.

"The phrase reflects our commitment to a core set of values inherited from generations before us, as well as our eagerness to put those beliefs into action today," says Jim Bush, chief executive officer. "The goals are high, the challenge is tough, and we're right on target."

Johnson & Galyon started in 1914 as the A.H. Whisman Company. In 1936, the firm incorporated, and the name was changed to Johnson & Willard in 1940, and to Johnson & Galyon in 1955.

Bush contends that the company's strength comes from its organizational structure. The current management team includes David Smith, president and chief operating officer; Mike Mauer, executive vice president; Ellen Fowler, vice president of administration; Steve Heatherly, vice president of marketing; and Susan Bacon, chief financial officer.

"We adhere to traditional values while being open to new processes," Bush says. "This brings both stability and judgment to our progressive company." As a result, Johnson & Galyon is responsible for many local landmarks, including the Whittle Building (the Howard Baker Federal Courthouse), the Riverview Tower, Knoxville's Riverfront Volunteer Landing, and the Knoxville Civic Auditorium and Coliseum.

Focused on East Tennessee

According to Bush, Johnson & Galyon has chosen to work exclusively on East Tennessee projects, rather than seeking projects in other parts of the country. "That means we work hard at keeping our clients satisfied," he says.

Repeat customers comprise a large portion of the firm's business. Johnson & Galyon has built the original structures and numerous additions at Baptist Hospital of East Tennessee and at Fort Sanders Medical Center and Children's Hospital. Kimberly-Clark Corporation, US Cellular, Cherokee Country Club, Medic Regional Blood Center, Lawler-Wood, and White Lily Foods are other repeat customers.

One of the most visible Johnson & Galyon projects has been the renovation of the downtown Miller's

Building for the Knoxville Utility Board (KUB). Beginning with a feasibility study for the City of Knoxville, Johnson & Galyon provided the expertise to return this historic building to its original grandeur. First, the company removed the building's glass skin, and then the firm repaired decades of neglect. Finally, Johnson & Galyon created an aesthetically pleasing interior and exterior true to the building's original character.

Today, Johnson & Galyon enjoys a long-term relationship with KUB. The firm has also renovated KUB facilities in West Knoxville and constructed new KUB facilities in East Knoxville.

"Many of our clients have demonstrated confidence in us by allowing us to do work for them again and again," says Bush. "As a result, you can't drive around town without seeing a building Johnson & Galyon has been involved with."

Similarly, there are few service organizations in East Tennessee that have not been touched either by financial contributions from Johnson & Galyon employees or by their active service. The list covers more than 20 local and regional nonprofit organizations.

"We live in East Tennessee; we build in East Tennessee," Bush says. "We're proud of our community and our role in its development."

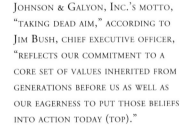

Johnson & Galyon, Inc.'s motto, "taking dead aim," according to Jim Bush, chief executive officer, "reflects our commitment to a core set of values inherited from generations before us as well as our eagerness to put those beliefs into action today (top)."

Johnson & Galyon, which adheres to traditional values while also being open to new processes, is responsible for many local landmarks in the East Tennessee area (bottom).

SOME 70 YEARS AGO IN 1930, THE SISTERS OF MERCY WERE ASKED TO BUILD A HOSPITAL IN EAST TENNESSEE, AND THE FUNDAMENTAL PURPOSE OF THE HOSPITAL REMAINS THE SAME TODAY. "OUR MISSION IS TO CARE FOR THE COMMUNITY, LARGELY THROUGH CARE OF THE SICK," EXPLAINS SISTER ELIZABETH RINEY, SENIOR VICE PRESIDENT OF CORPORATE MISSION FOR ST. MARY'S HEALTH SYSTEM. ■ BY PROVIDING QUALITY, COMPASSIONATE

health care for the community, especially for those who are poor and underserved, St. Mary's has become an integral part of the East Tennessee community. "Through letters, phone calls, and conversations with our patients, we have been told over and over again that we provide a high quality of care," Riney says. "The fact that we have been a witness to God's healing love for more than 70 years is another indication of our success."

Growing with the Community

As it has provided this quality health care, St. Mary's has also remained on the cutting edge of medicine. The area's first open-heart surgery was performed at St. Mary's, which also opened the region's first intensive care unit and ushered in a new era of childbirth when the Women's Pavilion opened. In addition, the hospital is the site of the first fully accredited member of the American Sleep Disorder Association in East Tennessee.

The hospital has grown from its original 63 beds and 12 bassinets to accommodate some 500 beds. St. Mary's Health System also comprises a number of satellite facilities, including 13 physician offices, a residential hospice, an assisted living facility, LaFollette Medical Center in Campbell County, Jefferson Memorial Hospital in Jefferson City, and a health and fitness center. New endeavors include a HUD-sponsored housing complex for low-income elderly and a new Jefferson Memorial Hospital. In addition, the organization's Web site—www.stmaryshealth.com—offers comprehensive health information, including the Eat Hearty! program that offers healthy recipes and a way to find healthy food when eating out.

"With all of our comprehensive health care services, it is our religious mission that sets us apart," Riney says. "We focus on continuing the healing ministry of Jesus, with emphasis on the poor and underserved. The presence of the Sisters of Mercy sets us apart. From the very beginning, St. Mary's has attracted and continues to attract excellent medical staff. We're blessed with the best medical staff in Knoxville."

Community Contributions

St. Mary's contributes more than $15 million annually to care for the poor and underserved. In addition, the organization supports more than 100 community agencies in East Tennessee. The health system's associates volunteer more than 11,000 hours each year to various community organizations as well.

Along with its corporate parent, Catholic Healthcare Partners, St. Mary's has established four key performance areas: cultural integration and enhancement, operational innovations to improve quality and reduce cost, partnering the creation of value-based integrated health systems, and community health improvement.

"St. Mary's continues to be very innovative in response to community needs," Riney says. "We're here to serve the people and to provide compassionate care to them when they have to be in our hospital. We're proud of carrying out the healing ministry of Jesus for the people of our community."

"OUR MISSION IS TO CARE FOR THE COMMUNITY, LARGELY THROUGH CARE OF THE SICK," EXPLAINS SISTER ELIZABETH RINEY, SENIOR VICE PRESIDENT OF CORPORATE MISSION FOR ST. MARY'S HEALTH SYSTEM.

Covenant Health

THANKS TO THE HEALTH CARE PROVIDERS AT COVENANT HEALTH, COMMU-NITIES AND FAMILIES THROUGHOUT EAST TENNESSEE ARE ENJOYING BETTER LIVES THROUGH BETTER HEALTH. LIVES ARE SAVED BY ADVANCED NEW TREATMENTS AT COVENANT HEALTH HOSPITALS AND SPECIALIZED CENTERS OF MEDICAL EXCELLENCE. HEALTH PROBLEMS ARE CAUGHT IN TIME BY FREE SCREENINGS AND EDUCATION. SHATTERED LIVES ARE RESTORED THROUGH

rehabilitation and behavioral health programs.

"At Covenant Health, we serve the community by improving the quality of life through better health," says Tony Spezia, president and CEO. "We provide programs to keep people healthy and we are constantly raising the bar to improve medical care in East Tennessee."

Spezia says that Covenant Health has developed a system of community health initiatives and preventive programs to help make a real impact on community and individual health. Covenant Health's free screenings and outreach programs reach thousands of people each year, promoting better health and wellness among children, adults, and seniors. "We believe that helping people maintain good health is as important to a community's well-being as treatment of disease and illness," Spezia says.

"AT COVENANT HEALTH, WE SERVE THE COMMUNITY BY IMPROVING THE QUALITY OF LIFE THROUGH BETTER HEALTH," SAYS TONY SPEZIA, PRESIDENT AND CEO (TOP).

OLYMPIC ATHLETE MISSY KANE NOW SERVES AS COVENANT HEALTH'S WELL-NESS SPOKESPERSON, HELPING PEOPLE GET IN SHAPE THROUGH WALKING PRO-GRAMS, PUBLIC TALKS, MEDIA EVENTS, AND OTHER CAUSES (BOTTOM).

Community-Owned Health Organization

Covenant Health's comprehensive services range from preventive care and education to open-heart surgery and cancer research. The health care delivery system includes six acute care hospitals, an inpatient psychiatric hospital, dozens of outpatient facilities, two outpatient cancer centers, specialized care in areas such as rehabilitation and senior health, physician and specialty clinics, and home health care. The organization boasts approximately 1,500 licensed beds, 8,500 employees, and 1,700 physicians.

"Our health professionals work together to provide the highest quality of care possible, and our organization exists to make sure this care is available and delivered in the most efficient and appropriate settings," Spezia says. "We are a strong, community-based health organization committed to building upon our reputation for quality, value, and excellence."

Spezia notes that Covenant Health is a not-for-profit health care organization with assets that belong to the communities it serves. "We have no shareholders looking for bottom-line profits," he explains. "Our earnings

are reinvested to improve local health services."

One of the First Hospitals in Knoxville

Chartered in 1919, Fort Sanders Regional Medical Center was the anchor hospital from which Fort Sanders Health System developed. The 562-bed facility is a regional referral center for neurosurgery, neurological disorders, orthopedics, oncology, cardiology, obstetrics, and rehabilitation medicine. The hospital also has a sleep disorders center and a transitional care unit.

In 1996, Fort Sanders Health System and MMC Healthcare System, which operated Methodist Medical Center of Oak Ridge, consolidated to form Covenant Health. The hospital originally opened in 1943 to serve the 80,000 men and women who came to Oak Ridge as part of the Manhattan Project. It was the home of many firsts, including nuclear medicine and intensive care units in Tennessee. The hospital has the highest percentage of board-certified physicians in the Knoxville area, and it was the first hospital to receive the Tennessee Quality Governor's Award.

Full Range of Health Care Services

Other acute care hospitals in the Covenant Health system include Fort Sanders Loudon Medical Center, Fort Sanders Parkwest Medical Center, Fort Sanders Sevier Medical Center, and Carthage General Hospital in Middle Tennessee. In addition, Covenant Health provides behavioral health services through Peninsula Hospital, Peninsula Village, and Peninsula Outpatient Centers.

Fort Sanders West, a Covenant Health facility, includes an outpatient surgery center, a diagnostic center, a diabetes center, a cardiopulmonary wellness and rehabilitation center, three medical office buildings, physical therapy and sports medicine, and a senior health center. Fort Sanders Health and Fitness Center and Nanny's Nursery are also located at Fort Sanders West.

Other Covenant Health facilities include the highly acclaimed Patricia Neal Rehabilitation Center, Thompson Cancer Survival Center, Methodist Regional Cancer Center, Covenant HomeCare, and Maternity Center of East Tennessee. Covenant Health also includes Covenant Medical Management, Inc., a physician practice management

organization, and the Fort Sanders Nursing Department at Tennessee Wesleyan College in Athens, which offers baccalaureate-level nursing education.

In addition, the company owns PHP Companies, Inc./Cariten Healthcare, which offers a variety of managed care insurance products and services. Cariten is one of East Tennessee's leading health insurance organizations and has more than 400,000 members.

"Our network of hospitals, physicians, outpatient care facilities, and specialties provide residents of East Tennessee with easy access to the medical care they need and ample locations and providers to choose from," Spezia says. "We are especially proud of our centers of excellence and services in the areas of cardiac care, cancer, stroke, rehabilitation, and maternity."

People Committed to Quality

The many faces of Covenant Health include a cadre of compassionate and dedicated physicians, nurses, technicians, therapists, and dietitians, as well as cooks, secretaries, information analysts, and teachers. They understand how important their work is, and share a unique sense of pride that comes from knowing their work touches the lives of so many families.

"Our employees are the backbone of our organization," Spezia says. "Together, they share their resources and expertise with East Tennessee. Together, they bring a commitment to high-quality health care into our communities."

EACH YEAR NEARLY 4,500 BABIES ARE BORN AT COVENANT HEALTH HOSPITALS.

COVENANT HEALTH EMPLOYEES DONATE MORE THAN 5,000 VOLUNTEER HOURS EACH YEAR TO NUMEROUS COMMUNITY SERVICE PROJECTS, SUCH AS BUILDING HOUSES FOR HABITAT FOR HUMANITY AND FITNESS TRAILS FOR SCHOOLCHILDREN.

Tennessee Valley Authority

CRAVEN CROWELL, CHAIRMAN OF THE TENNESSEE VALLEY AUTHORITY'S (TVA) THREE-MEMBER BOARD OF DIRECTORS, ASSERTS THAT "THE TENNESSEE VALLEY AUTHORITY HAS LONG BEEN AN INTEGRAL PART OF THE KNOXVILLE ECONOMY AND THE GREATER TENNESSEE VALLEY, WHICH IS NOW GROWING AT ALMOST TWICE THE NATIONAL RATE." ■ "BY SUPPLYING ONE OF THE MOST BASIC INGREDIENTS OF ECONOMIC GROWTH—LOW-COST, RELIABLE

electric power—TVA is a key partner in generating prosperity for the nearly 8 million people we serve," Crowell adds.

A federal corporation, TVA is the nation's largest public electricity producer, a regional economic development agency, and a steward of the Tennessee River basin. The U.S. Congress formed the organization in 1933, primarily to provide flood control, navigation, and electric power in the Tennessee Valley region. This region covers about 80,000 square miles in the southeastern United States, including most of Tennessee and parts of Alabama, Georgia, Kentucky, Mississippi, North Carolina, and Virginia.

TVA's generating facilities include three nuclear plants, 11 coal-fired plants, 29 hydroelectric dams, and a pumped storage facility. Together, they provide 29,469 megawatts. Coal-fired plants typically produce two-thirds of TVA's electricity, with nuclear and hydroelectric plants providing the balance.

TVA provides power to 158 local municipal and cooperative power distributors through a network of some 17,000 miles of transmission

lines. These local distributors then deliver power to homes, businesses, and industries. TVA also sells power directly to more than 60 large industrial customers and federal agencies.

Supplying Low-Cost, Reliable Power

Because TVA's core product is so essential to so many, the reliability and availability of our facilities are top priorities," Crowell emphasizes. "Through meticulous attention to maintenance and modernization, aggressive pursuit of greater productivity, and optimizing

the use of assets, TVA is able to ensure its plants are available when they are needed most."

To make such service possible, TVA has added base-load generating capacity over the years, and has plans to continue increasing capacity through improvements to existing units and the addition of peaking units. TVA has also been able to reliably meet the increasing demand for power because its systems are operating more efficiently than at any other time in the past three decades, according to Crowell. TVA increased output by about 20 percent from 1994 to 2000.

Perhaps most important, TVA has kept its rates down. The organization's power prices are among the most competitive in the nation, with residential prices 23 percent lower than the national average.

Stimulating Sustainable Economic Growth

Competitive rates for power are also a benefit to business and industry, giving communities in the Tennessee Valley an important tool for fostering new business investment in the area. TVA works closely with local power distributors and community leaders to develop innovative programs that are attracting quality investments.

Since 1995, TVA has offered more than $90 million in economic

THE TENNESSEE RIVER AND ITS TRIBUTARIES MAKE UP THE FIFTH-LARGEST RIVER SYSTEM IN THE NATION, INCLUDING SOME 800 MILES OF COMMERCIALLY NAVIGABLE RIVER.

development loans. These loans and other technical and economic development services have leveraged more than $1 billion in capital investment, and have helped to create and retain more than 230,000 jobs.

TVA's Comprehensive Services Program makes the organization's engineering and technical assistance to current or potential customers possible. TVA's Site Selector program is an information partnership with eight regional industrial development associations that help relocating businesses and industries find sites that best fit their needs. Small businesses are supported by 18 small-business incubators, jointly sponsored by TVA and local communities. Residential customers benefit from the *energy right* program, which offers a combination of low-interest loans and incentives for those who install heat pumps and who buy all-electric homes and energy-efficient manufactured homes.

"Electricity is such a fundamental part of everyday life that TVA's success in producing and transmitting power efficiently, without federal appropriations, translates directly into prosperity and jobs," Crowell says.

Supporting a Thriving River System

The Tennessee River and its tributaries make up the fifth-largest river system in the nation. The Tennessee River includes some 800 miles of commercially navigable river, with a 652-mile main channel from Knoxville to Paducah and 148 miles of tributary channels. In

managing this system, TVA fulfills flood-control and navigation commitments that greatly benefit the regional economy.

In addition, the demand for recreational use along the Tennessee River has steadily increased over the years. TVA reservoirs have a total surface area of some 480,000 acres and some 11,000 miles of shoreline. TVA operates about 100 recreation areas and helps to generate millions of recreation-related dollars annually for the region's economy.

Structuring for a Deregulated Environment

TVA is powerfully positioned, consistently competitive, and fiscally fit," Crowell says. Actively engaged in the national electrical utility restructuring debate, TVA is working to ensure that the new

system is, according to Crowell, "fair to public and private power; fair to all regions of the country; beneficial to private consumers as well as large customers; and compatible for all utilities' responsibilities to customers for reliability, universal access, environmental stewardship, and economic development."

"I believe the challenge for public utilities will be to continue to embrace the dual identity Franklin Roosevelt envisioned more than 60 years ago: Public in fact, private in behavior; solid and responsible, yet creative and competitive," Crowell asserts. "In this way, TVA and public utilities like ours will set a standard for public responsibility against which private companies can be measured, even as we continue to provide our core product at competitive prices."

TVA PROVIDES POWER TO 158 LOCAL MUNICIPAL AND COOPERATIVE POWER DISTRIBUTORS THROUGH A NETWORK OF SOME 17,000 MILES OF TRANSMISSION LINES.

Knoxville Utilities Board

FOR MORE THAN 60 YEARS, THE KNOXVILLE UTILITIES BOARD (KUB) HAS MET THE UTILITY NEEDS OF THE PEOPLE OF THE KNOXVILLE AREA. INCORPORATED AS A MUNICIPAL UTILITY IN 1939, KUB HAS GROWN OVER THE YEARS TO INCLUDE NOT ONLY ELECTRIC AND WATER SERVICE, BUT ALSO GAS AND WASTEWATER SERVICE. THROUGH THE YEARS, KUB'S FOCUS HAS ALWAYS BEEN ON PROVIDING THE BEST SERVICE TO ITS CUSTOMERS AT LOW RATES. THAT

THE KNOXVILLE UTILITIES BOARD (KUB) PROVIDES THE ENERGY TO LIGHT UP KNOXVILLE AND THE EXPERTISE TO HELP THE COMMUNITIES IN ITS SERVICE AREA GROW.

KUB HAS ALWAYS CALLED DOWNTOWN HOME AND IS HONORED TO HAVE ITS HEADQUARTERS IN ONE OF THE COMMUNITY'S MOST SIGNIFICANT LANDMARKS, THE MILLER'S BUILDING.

began in the first year of service, when customers of the Knoxville Electric Power and Water Board saved more than $1 million in rates, and it continues today. The financial plan adopted by the KUB Board of Commissioners in 2000 marked the fifth consecutive year of rate deferrals, saving the typical KUB customer $300 over the five-year period.

As it builds on the successes of its past, KUB is also retooling itself for a future filled with challenges. With deregulation of the electric industry predicted for the early part of the new century, utilities across the country have had to change their operations to be more sensitive to customer needs, and more efficient and effective in the delivery of utility services. KUB is no different.

Over the past several years, KUB's employees have focused on four corporate objectives: do the basics better, be more customer focused, be environmentally responsible, and support the community's growth. KUB's employees have found that accomplishing these objectives is what sets their company apart from its

peers in the utility industry. They have made KUB a leader in preparing for the future.

Do the Basics Better

KUB's employees have spent the past several years making changes to processes in construction, customer service, operations, and support activities to ensure high levels of service to customers, as well as low rates. The changes have made the company more efficient and have saved hundreds of thousands of dollars in the process. But low rates will not be enough in the competitive world to come; customer expectations must still be met, and all of KUB's efforts to do the basics better must be coupled with an appreciation of those expectations.

Be More Customer Focused

KUB significantly improved its services over the years. Many of those decisions were made based on a basic understanding of what most customers wanted. The new KUB, however, has recognized that all customers are not alike: each desires different things and different ways of doing business. That's why KUB has begun to ask customers directly what they expect from their utility. Results of surveys and focus groups have helped KUB to develop programs that are responsive to the specific needs of different kinds of customers.

Major industrial customers want a single point of contact to talk to about any KUB issue; developers and contractors want an efficient process to use when ordering new services; residential customers want more information about KUB projects in their neighborhoods; and all require different kinds of services. KUB is working hard to meet those needs.

Be Environmentally Responsible

As a municipal utility, KUB believes strongly in being a good steward of our natural resources. The company not only complies with environmental regulations, but also goes above and beyond these rules, when possible, to ensure that its services are sensitive to environmental concerns. KUB is proud of its performance in this area.

The company's state-of-the-art water laboratory conducts more than 90,000 tests a year of the water and wastewater systems. Water quality is critical to the life of any community, and KUB is proud to report that it has always met or exceeded state and federal drinking water standards. KUB participates in local advocacy groups and outreach activities to help promote clean water, and, in 2000, was awarded the Directors Certificate of Recognition from the Partnership for Safe Water for its efforts to optimize plant operations.

In 2000, KUB—in partnership with TVA—introduced Green Power Switch, a pilot program that allows customers to choose environmentally friendly energy sources. KUB has always taken its environmental responsibilities seriously and will continue to do so.

Support the Community's Growth

Perhaps KUB's most important objective is to support the community's growth. The company accomplishes this in many ways—whether it is extending new services for new development, relocating a major network substation on an expedited schedule to accommodate construction of the new convention center, or facilitating a grant to a major industrial customer to keep jobs in the inner city. Perhaps the most visible investment in the community in 2000 was the renovation of the Miller's Building on Gay Street in downtown Knoxville. This building, a Knoxville landmark since about 1900, was months away from the wrecking ball when KUB partnered with the City of Knoxville to renovate and restore it. Now, the build-

ing has reclaimed its landmark status, serving as KUB's corporate headquarters and providing additional floor space for new tenants in the downtown area. Recruiting new tenants to downtown in that office space is yet another way KUB is helping to support the community.

KUB has had the privilege of serving the Knoxville area for decades. Its challenge for the years to come is to live up to the success of the past and the ever rising expectations of its customers. Through a continual focus on improvement, KUB's employees plan to do just that.

Blount Memorial Occupational Health

T IS GENERALLY ACCEPTED THAT A COMPANY'S FISCAL CONDITION IS DIRECTLY LINKED TO ITS EMPLOYEES' PHYSICAL CONDITION. WHEN EMPLOYEES HAVE IMMEDIATE ACCESS TO TREATMENT AND REHABILITATION FOR ON-THE-JOB INJURIES AND PREVENTIVE HEALTH SCREENINGS THAT HELP DETECT POTENTIAL HEALTH PROBLEMS, PRODUCTIVITY INCREASES AND THE NUMBER OF LOST WORKDAYS DECREASES. THE bottom line is that good health is good for business.

Since 1947, Blount Memorial Occupational Health has been making sense for area industries and companies because it creates cost-effective and efficient occupational health programs for corporate clients throughout East Tennessee. The organization's one-stop-shop approach to occupational health eliminates the need to contract with multiple entities for separate health care services, and the menu of options gives employers the flexibility to choose only the services their company requires. Affiliation with Blount Memorial Hospital ensures that employees will have access to state-of-the-art technology, top physicians, and comprehensive services.

On-Site Nursing

Clients of Blount Memorial Occupational Health can select from a variety of options, including on-site nursing care, return-to-work follow-up, and assistance with completing workers' compensation and medical claims. An on-site nurse is an occupational health professional who handles all emergencies, conducts any necessary follow-up care, and performs regular assessments by observing employees at work.

The on-site nursing option decreases sick time and health care costs by reducing the number of visits to the emergency room or urgent care clinic. And when employers ask Blount Memorial Occupational Health to take care of the time-consuming paperwork involved with workers' compensation cases and medical claims, they have more time to focus on what they do best—operating their business.

Consultation and Education

Blount Memorial Occupational Health's menu of services available to companies includes health and safety programs, health screenings, personal health education, and consultation services. For example, the organization offers innovative health and safety programs tailored to meet a company's specific needs, including American Red Cross CPR and first aid, back injuries education, blood pressure tracking, cumulative trauma prevention, and exposure control training. In addition, by offering voluntary health screenings such as hypertension and cancer screenings to employees, Blount Memorial can help detect early symptoms of disease or illness and reduce long-term health care expense.

There are currently two state-of-the-art Blount Memorial Occupational Health Centers conveniently located for business and industry in the Knoxville area. One is in Alcoa at the Blount Memorial Health Center at Springbrook; the other is in Vonore at the Blount Memorial Health Center at Tellico West. At these centers, a variety of occupational health services are available, including preplacement examinations, on-the-job injury evaluations, drug and alcohol testing, ergonomic evaluations, compliance with OSHA regulations, and immediate treatment for short-term, on-the-job illnesses and injuries.

In addition to specific occupational health services, clients who partner with Blount Memorial Hospital have access to a wide range of programs, including work hardening, rehabilitation, employee assistance, and wellness. Whether a company requires a comprehensive occupational health program or has a specific occupational health problem to solve, Blount Memorial Occupational Health works to improve a company's business by improving its employees' health. Cost-effective, efficient, and expert at keeping workers healthy and on the job, the organization is truly a boon to the area and to its workforce.

BLOUNT MEMORIAL OCCUPATIONAL HEALTH CREATES COST-EFFECTIVE AND EFFICIENT OCCUPATIONAL HEALTH PROGRAMS FOR CORPORATE CLIENTS THROUGHOUT EAST TENNESSEE.

NSTRUMENTATION DESIGNED AND MANUFACTURED BY ZELLWEGER USTER, INC. IS BEING USED TO TEST AND CLASS ALL OF THE COTTON PRODUCED IN THE UNITED STATES, AS WELL AS MUCH OF THE COTTON AND OTHER FIBERS PRODUCED WORLDWIDE. FOR THIS REASON, KNOXVILLE IS THE FIBER-TESTING CAPITAL OF THE WORLD. ■ "USTER INSTRUMENTATION CAN BE FOUND AT EVERY LEVEL OF COTTON PRODUCTION," SAYS HOSSEIN GHORASHI,

Zellweger Uster, Inc.

interim president and CEO of Zellweger Uster. "As cotton is ginned and baled, our instruments monitor and control the process to proactively improve fiber quality and production efficiencies. As the cotton is spun into yarn, our instruments measure the fiber properties and monitor the production machinery. As the yarn is woven into fabrics, our instruments ensure the efficiency of the looms. In every step of cotton production, our instruments are there, making sure that the quality of the end product is the best that it can possibly be."

Global Structure

With corporate headquarters in Knoxville and a sales and service office in Charlotte, Zellweger Uster is part of a much larger team. Knoxville's 120 employees are part of the 5,000-employee, $700 million Zellweger Luwa Group based in Switzerland. The corporate parent is a diversified and decentralized enterprise that operates in nearly every country around the globe.

The company ventured into the U.S. market in 1948, when the Uster Corporation was established in Charlotte to investigate the postwar opportunities offered by the American textile industry. The company's first electronic product, the Evenness Tester, gave mills a technological edge in the measurement of yarn quality.

Also in 1948, a company called Special Instruments Laboratory, or Spinlab, was forming in Knoxville as a result of technology related to the Manhattan Project during World War II. Instruments were invented to measure cotton length and fineness, and to perform basic research in the measurement of physical properties of cotton fibers.

Convergence of Capabilities

Zellweger Uster, which over the years has added several companies to its holdings, acquired Spinlab in 1990. "Similar to the con-

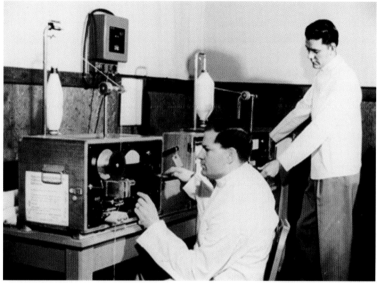

fluence of a river, our strength comes from varying paths," Ghorashi says.

"Our testimony is in our achievements," Ghorashi continues. "We are now the world leader in quality systems for the textile industry, accounting for a market share above 90 percent. The newest addition to our product line is breaking new ground. The IntelliGin has the capacity to revolutionize the ginning industry, with the potential to increase the total cotton economy by $1 billion."

More than 40 patents have been granted to Zellweger Uster's Knoxville office. The company's staff includes researchers, physicists, engineers, and electronics experts. The firm's marketing executives, product managers, and product support employees travel around the world from their base in Knoxville to educate, train, and service customers.

Approximately 80 percent of the products Zellweger Uster manufactures in Knoxville are exported, and the U.S. Department of Agriculture Cotton Program is the company's largest customer. Other customers include research institutions, universities, and textile manufacturers.

Although its market is global, Zellweger Uster focuses locally when it comes to giving back to the community. The company's Knoxville

employees support such programs as United Way, as well as various cultural and educational programs throughout the community. Through their efforts, more than $100,000 is invested back into the community each year, Ghorashi says. Focus on industry and community makes Zellweger Uster, Inc. a boon to the Knoxville area.

Baptist Health System

BY OFFERING SPECIALIZED SERVICES AND INDIVIDUALIZED PATIENT CARE, BAPTIST HEALTH SYSTEM MEETS THE UNIQUE HEALTH CARE NEEDS OF EAST TENNESSEANS. NAMED ONE OF THE TOP 100 HOSPITALS IN THE NATION FOR THREE YEARS IN A ROW, BAPTIST'S FLAGSHIP HOSPITAL—BAPTIST HOSPITAL OF EAST TENNESSEE—PROVIDES INNOVATIVE TREATMENTS AND COMPRE-HENSIVE CARE. THE ONLY HEALTH SYSTEM IN TENNESSEE HONORED WITH

the prestigious Governor's Award for Quality and a Consumer Choice Award winner, Baptist Health System serves a 17-county region with experienced physicians and specialists who deliver the highest level of health care.

With Centers of Excellence in cancer, cardiology, pain management, senior care, and women's health, Baptist remains on the forefront of health care by offering advanced services. Baptist enters the new millennium dedicated to leadership, and with a vision of growth and a commitment to continued research.

"Baptist Health System's vision comes down to one thing—leadership," says Dale Collins, president and CEO. "We're leading the way toward better health for all East Tennesseans. No matter what may change in the new century, our commitment to leadership in health care is one thing that will ultimately stay the same."

A History of Caring

In 1942, a survey determined that Knoxville was 60 percent below the national average for available hospital beds. A group of dedicated Baptists organized their resources and received a charter from the State of Tennessee to establish a hospital in

1943. Baptist Hospital admitted its first patient in maternity on November 26, 1948. During its first year, Baptist admitted some 7,700 patients and more than 1,100 babies were delivered.

Baptist Hospital grew through the years, with the addition of the Blount Professional Building, followed by the Graves-Wyatt Chapel, Baptist Professional Building, Baptist Heart Institute, and Baptist Eye Institute. Baptist Hospital of Cocke County became a part of Baptist Health System in the 1980s. Expanded services include seven senior health centers, outpatient radiation centers in Morristown and Harrogate, and health information centers located in two area malls.

In 1991, the hospital underwent an $8 million expansion program to upgrade outpatient services, adding new operating rooms and building a crossover between the hospital and the parking garage. The Baptist Medical Tower, a $14 million project, opened in 1993. Today, the hospital complex is a major landmark on the Knoxville riverfront.

Specialized Services

As one of the top 100 cardiovascular facilities in the nation, Baptist Heart Institute provides the necessary resources to fight the area's number one killer, heart disease. Baptist Heart Institute is home to a hypertension center, a cardiac rehabili-

tation program, a chest pain emergency center, a network of the area's best cardiologists, community outreach programs, and the latest technology, including new lifesaving surgical procedures such as TMR—which is a laser heart surgery—and minimally invasive heart surgery.

A leader in clinical trials, affiliated with Vanderbilt-Ingram Cancer Center, and chosen to conduct research with the nation's top cancer centers, the Baptist Regional Cancer Center works to ensure that aggressive, effective treatment is always available in Knoxville. A team of oncologists, hematologists, radiation oncologists, and gynecologic oncologists deliver lifesaving treatments. From radiation therapy, chemotherapy, and surgery to early detection techniques, Baptist offers the technology needed to increase the chances of survival.

Baptist is ready to meet the growing needs of the aging population. By providing more specialized services geared to treat osteoporosis, mental health, and caregiving issues, Baptist helps keep seniors secure, safe, and healthy in the comfort of their own homes. Baptist offers the area's first fellowship-trained geriatrician, seven senior health centers delivering primary health care services especially for those 55 and over, the area's largest senior benefits program, the Geriatric Assessment Program, the Senior Life Skills Program, and the Senior Dynamics Unit.

BAPTIST HOSPITAL OF EAST TENNESSEE IS THE FLAGSHIP OF BAPTIST HEALTH SYSTEM. NAMED ONE OF THE TOP 100 HOSPITALS IN THE NATION, BAPTIST STRIVES TO EXCEED THE EXPECTATIONS OF EAST TENNESSEE BY DELIVERING SUPERIOR HEALTH CARE SERVICES (TOP).

BY OFFERING RADIOLOGICAL SERVICES AND CHEMOTHERAPY, AS WELL AS PAR-TICIPATING IN NUMEROUS CLINICAL TRIALS, THE BAPTIST REGIONAL CANCER CENTER IS STAYING A STEP AHEAD OF CANCER (BOTTOM).

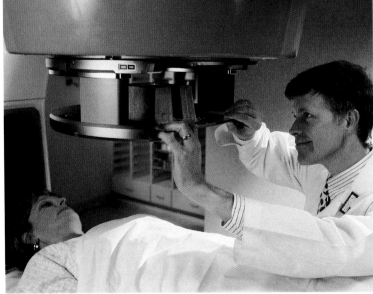

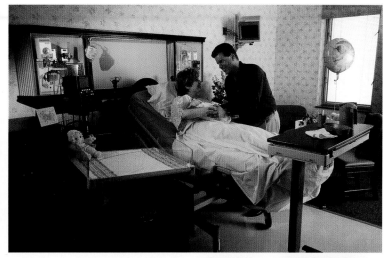

As the area's most comprehensive chronic pain management center, the Baptist Pain Institute provides medical treatment for benign and malignant pain. Chronic pain specialists work with nurse practitioners, physical therapy personnel, and support staff to stay on the leading edge of pain treatment. Whether pain stems from illnesses, accidents, injuries, or debilitating diseases, the Baptist Pain Institute offers the treatments needed to ease symptoms.

Baptist knows that women have special, unique health concerns. By offering the Women's Imaging Center, which includes mammography and ultrasound; the Clayton Birthing Center; a dedicated team of obstetrician/gynecologists; early osteoporosis detection; dermatology services; and breast and gynecologic cancer specialties, Baptist is a leader in women's health care.

Additional services include the Sleep Disorders Center, the Diabetes Treatment Center, a 24-hour-a-day ASK-A-NURSE health information and physician referral line, Home Health, Hospice and Rehabilitation.

West Knoxville Expansion

Baptist recognizes the need to grow and expand in the new millennium. With more people moving into the Greater Knoxville area, the hospital has initiated plans to provide access to its services in those areas that are seeing a growth in population.

Two new developments are slated to open in the near future on the site of the Turkey Creek development. Baptist Hospital-West is a 75-bed hospital providing inpatient and out-patient services, an emergency room, cardiac catheterization, radiation oncology, imaging, and other services. At the Baptist Women's Hospital, 16 suites for labor and delivery, surgery, gynecology, and other services will be available along with physician offices.

"In the future, our tradition of delivering quality health care will continue to grow in new neighborhoods," Collins says. "Now more than ever before, we have the ability to help Knoxvillians live longer, healthier lives thanks to better programs, convenient locations, and new medications, surgical procedures, and treatments."

BAPTIST'S CLAYTON BIRTHING CENTER PROVIDES COMFORTABLE, HOMELIKE DELIVERY ROOMS WHERE MOM, DAD, AND BABY CAN FEEL SAFE AND SECURE (TOP LEFT).

PATIENTS 55 AND OLDER RECEIVE PRIMARY CARE PHYSICIAN SERVICES AT SEVEN BAPTIST SENIOR HEALTH CENTER LOCATIONS (TOP RIGHT).

BAPTIST'S COMPREHENSIVE WOMEN'S IMAGING CENTER OFFERS MAMMOGRAPHY, ULTRASOUND, AND OTHER DIAGNOSTIC PROCEDURES (CENTER).

AS ONE OF THE TOP 100 CARDIOVASCULAR PROGRAMS IN THE NATION, THE BAPTIST HEART INSTITUTE OFFERS A COMPLETE RANGE OF SERVICES, INCLUDING A CARDIAC REHABILITATION PROGRAM AND THE LATEST SURGICAL PROCEDURES (BELOW LEFT).

A COMPREHENSIVE PAIN MANAGEMENT FACILITY, THE BAPTIST PAIN INSTITUTE STAYS ON THE LEADING EDGE OF CHRONIC PAIN TREATMENT (BELOW RIGHT).

Campbell, Cunningham & Taylor, P.C.

SINCE 1949, CAMPBELL, CUNNINGHAM & TAYLOR, P.C. HAS BROUGHT EXTENSIVE AND INNOVATIVE EYE CARE TO THE KNOXVILLE AREA. THIS SOLID TRADITION HAS BEEN MADE POSSIBLE BY A PROGRESSIVE PHILOSOPHY OF CARE, WHICH HAS, IN MANY CASES, REVOLUTIONIZED THE WAY EYE PROBLEMS ARE TREATED. "WE ARE TOTALLY COMMITTED TO EXCELLENCE IN SERVICE AND THE APPLICATION OF TECHNOLOGY," SAYS PHILIP D. Campbell, M.D., son of one of the firm's founders. "Using lasers, surgical microscopes, microsurgical instruments, diagnostic computers, and ultrasound, the doctors and staff are among the best in eye care available to the area."

In addition to Campbell, the practice is supported by more than 25 years' cumulative experience in ophthalmology with partners Leslie B. Cunningham, M.D., and C. Tobin Taylor, M.D. Each doctor is similarly board certified in ophthalmology. In addition to general ophthalmology, the doctors specialize in laser vision correction, cataract microsurgery, eyelid plastic surgery, treatments of dry eyes, glaucoma, and disease and surgery of the eye.

In 1996, the group created the Eye Surgery Center of East Tennessee, a specialized outpatient ophthalmic surgery facility. Less than a year later, The Campbell Cunningham Laser Center was established, becoming Knoxville's first laser vision correction center with an on-site excimer laser. In fact, Campbell performed Knoxville's first laser-assisted in situ keratomileusis (LASIK) procedure in fall 1996. Since then, Campbell and Cunningham have become the first doctors in the Southeast to perform such a procedure on live broadcast television.

"In designing these two centers, our goal was to provide patients with convenient access to advanced care delivered in facilities that are equipped and staffed especially for those services," Cunningham says.

The Campbell Cunningham Laser Center is a combination of years of experience with the advanced excimer laser to provide the LASIK procedure for correcting nearsightedness, farsightedness, and astigmatism. This procedure allows a tremendous amount of precision, control, and safety in the surgical correction of vision errors.

LASIK has already benefited thousands of patients at The Campbell Cunningham Laser Center. "The majority of our patients are able to return to work and even drive the day following the procedure," Cunningham adds.

Another specialty of the practice is cataract microsurgery. A

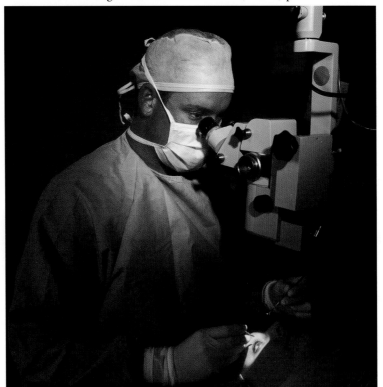

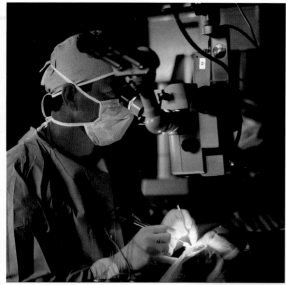
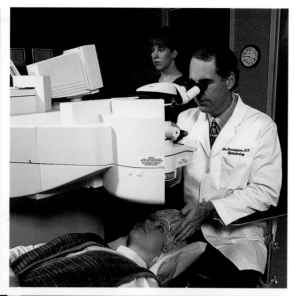

cataract is a progressive clouding of the eye's natural lens that interferes with light passing through to the retina. More than 50 percent of people over the age of 60—and quite a few who are younger—suffer from cataracts. This microsurgery is performed on an outpatient basis and takes only a few minutes. According to the American Society of Cataract and Refractive Surgery, more than 98 percent of all cataract patients reported that their vision successfully improved after surgery.

At Campbell, Cunningham & Taylor, P.C., clients are assured of receiving eye care that is among the finest available in the Knoxville area. Each of the firm's doctors is experienced, credentialed, and reputable.

A graduate of Tulane School of Medicine and Emory University, Campbell is certified by the American Board of Ophthalmology and the American Board of Eye Surgery. He specializes primarily in laser vision correction, as well as cataract, intraocular lens, anterior segment microsurgery, glaucoma, and diabetic eye disease management.

Certified by the American Board of Pediatrics and the American Board of Ophthalmology, Cunningham is a graduate of the University of Mississippi School of Medicine. He specializes in laser vision correction and also in cataract and intraocular lens surgery, anterior segment microsurgery, glaucoma, and diabetic eye disease management.

Taylor graduated with highest honors from Baylor College of

Medicine and is certified by the American Board of Ophthalmology. He specializes in cataract and various microsurgery procedures, glaucoma and diabetic eye disease management, neuro-ophthalmology, and eyelid and lacrimal surgery.

With Campbell, Cunningham & Taylor, P.C.; Eye Surgery Center of East Tennessee; and The Campbell Cunningham Laser Center, patients can receive the most complete eye care available under one roof.

PHILIP D. CAMPBELL, M.D. (TOP LEFT AND CENTER) AND LESLIE B. CUNNINGHAM, M.D. (TOP RIGHT) SPECIALIZE IN LASER VISION CORRECTION, AS WELL AS HAVING OTHER AREAS OF SPECIALTY.

THE PRACTICE IS SUPPORTED BY MORE THAN 25 YEARS' CUMULATIVE EXPERIENCE IN OPHTHALMOLOGY, AND ALMOST 15 YEARS IN OPTOMETRY BY C. ALLYN HILDEBRAND, O.D.

1950-1979

1953
WATE-TV

1954
Arnett, Draper and Hagood

1956
The University of Tennessee Medical Center

1957
Rice Automotive Group

1958
Cherokee Distributing Company

1968
Bandit Lites, Inc.

1972
Hyatt Regency Knoxville

1974
Pellissippi State Technical Community College

1979
Knoxville Convention and Visitors Bureau

1979
The Transition Team

WATE-TV

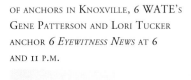

ITHIN THE WALLS OF A 19TH-CENTURY LANDMARK, 21ST-CENTURY TECHNOLOGY IS USED TO INFORM AND ENTERTAIN EAST TENNESSEANS. 6 WATE WAS KNOXVILLE'S FIRST TV STATION. FOR NEARLY 50 YEARS, IT HAS BEEN AN INNOVATOR, LEADER, AND TRUSTED SOURCE FOR QUALITY PROGRAMMING AND COMMUNITY SERVICE. UNDER THE OWNERSHIP OF YOUNG BROADCASTING, INC., THAT COMMITMENT CONTINUES TODAY.

WATE-TV began as WROL-TV, with its first telecast on October 1, 1953. From the beginning, the station pioneered local programs that served the community, including *Mary Starr's Homemaker Show* and *TV Classroom Quiz.*

6 WATE quickly outgrew its facilities in those early years. In 1962, the station purchased and restored Greystone, a mansion built for Major Eldad Cicero Camp, a Union officer in the Civil War, as well as a Knoxville lawyer and entrepreneur. The building is said to be an exact duplicate of President James A. Garfield's home in Washington, D.C.

Today, Greystone is listed on the National Register of Historic Places

and is home to more than 100 employees of 6 WATE. Additions to the building provide room for a state-of-the-art newsroom, a large production studio, and high-tech equipment such as satellite uplinks, all necessary to keep 6 WATE on the air 24 hours a day.

One of the latest technological advances housed at Greystone is the 6 Storm Team Weather Lab. Chief Meteorologist Matt Hinkin—recognized as one of the area's most trusted meteorologists—and his staff gather and communicate vital weather information from this unique facility. In the weather lab are a dozen computers, Doppler Radar, Stormtracker, and 6 WATE's latest innovation,

Instant WeatherNet. With Instant WeatherNet, the 6 Storm Team and viewers can see weather conditions data, like temperature, wind speed, and precipitation, in real time from several East Tennessee locations.

6 WATE was the first TV station to embrace the Internet as a way to communicate information to the public. The station's Web site, www.wate.com, was also the first in Knoxville to provide locally reported news whenever it breaks; complete weather information; and thorough, in-depth coverage of high school sports.

As broadcast television moves from analog to digital technology, 6 WATE will continue to lead the way. Years before a new tower was constructed and a digital transmitter was installed, the station had already invested hundreds of thousands of dollars in digital equipment for news gathering and broadcast. It was the first area TV station to equip a truck with a digital satellite uplink dish to bring news coverage to East Tennessee from anywhere in the country.

News Leadership

Nowhere is 6 WATE's commitment to the community and tradition of excellence more evident than in its news broadcasts. *6 Eyewitness News* is "coverage you can count on," a statement that is more than a slogan. It's a demonstration of how the news station provides reliable, accurate information that viewers find useful and meaningful.

For five decades, *6 Eyewitness News* has been a leader in covering important news, like education, medical breakthroughs, consumer issues, and weather. One special feature of the news broadcasts is 6 On Your Side. In these reports, Don Dare investigates government waste, scams, and rip-offs, and serves as a troubleshooter for consumer complaints. *6 Eyewitness News* is also the only local newscast to regularly

ONE OF THE MOST EXPERIENCED TEAMS OF ANCHORS IN KNOXVILLE, 6 WATE'S GENE PATTERSON AND LORI TUCKER ANCHOR *6 EYEWITNESS NEWS* AT 6 AND 11 P.M.

cover educational issues that affect the community.

In recent years, *6 Eyewitness News* has been honored with several prestigious awards. The Society for Professional Journalists, Radio Television News Directors Association, National Academy of Television Arts and Sciences, and Associated Press Broadcasters have all presented the program with awards for excellence in journalism, including several coveted Edward R. Murrow Regional awards. In 2000, *6 Eyewitness News* was the only Knoxville TV station to win a Murrow award and the only news station in its region to win three.

In addition to awards from its broadcasting peers, 6 WATE has been honored by many national and local public service agencies, community groups, and charitable organizations. Among them are the Gabriel Award from the National Catholic Association of Communicators and the Russell L. Cecil Award for the Southeastern Region from the Arthritis Foundation.

Trusted Community Member

6 WATE makes a special effort to cover community issues and needs in its newscasts, programming, and public service announcements. It is the only local station offering weekly commentaries that address political and governmental issues.

6 WATE also broadcasts *Tennessee This Week*, a weekly half-hour program of information and viewpoints of local interest.

For more than a decade, *New at the Zoo* has entertained and educated children and adults. It is a weekly program hosted by Hinkin and Tim Adams, Knoxville Zoo's director of zoo education. No other TV station in the Southeast produces and broadcasts a regularly scheduled program like it.

6 WATE also shows its commitment to children and parents with *Children First*, which combines news reports, public service announcements, and quarterly public affairs specials. Parenting and important issues that affect the well-being of children are explored in this project.

In addition, 6 WATE helps in public education and awareness throughout the year by airing telethons, public service campaigns, and special programs. Important issues like education, downtown development, and medical advances have been explored in these efforts. Of particular note is 6 WATE's support of Second Harvest Food Bank. In recent years, more than 1 million pounds of food have been collected through events associated with the 6 Shares Food Drive.

From its beginning as WROL, WATE-TV is continuing to grow in the Knoxville area and beyond. With ever changing technology innovations, the station is sure to move into the future with considerable speed.

GREYSTONE, BUILT FOR MAJOR ELDAD CICERO CAMP IN 1890, WAS BOUGHT AND RESTORED BY WATE-TV IN THE 1960S, WHEN IT WAS CONVERTED INTO OFFICES AND PRODUCTION STUDIOS.

6 WATE'S CHIEF METEOROLOGIST, MATT HINKIN, IS ONE OF THE AREA'S MOST TRUSTED METEOROLOGISTS.

Arnett, Draper and Hagood

A COMMITMENT TO EXCELLENCE MAY BEST DESCRIBE THE PHILOSOPHY OF ARNETT, DRAPER AND HAGOOD. THE FIRM OCCUPIES THE 23RD FLOOR OF THE FIRST TENNESSEE PLAZA IN KNOXVILLE, AND IS COUNSEL TO APPROXIMATELY 1,000 PERSONAL AND CORPORATE CLIENTS IN ALL AREAS OF CIVIL LAW. ■ THIS LAW FIRM WAS FOUNDED IN 1954 BY FOSTER D. ARNETT. JACK B. DRAPER JOINED ARNETT IN 1958, AND LEWIS R. HAGOOD

became a member of the firm seven years later. Today, 21 lawyers are in the firm's portfolio of professional services. These areas of practice include labor and employment discrimination law; hospital and health care; wills; trusts and estates; estate litigation; sale and acquisition of businesses and properties; and tort liability, including appellate practice in state and federal courts. Other areas of practice include ERISA law, workers' compensation law, aviation law, malpractice claims, and civil and corporate litigation.

THE LAW FIRM OF ARNETT, DRAPER AND HAGOOD WAS FOUNDED IN 1954 BY FOSTER D. ARNETT (CENTER), WHO WAS JOINED BY JACK B. DRAPER (LEFT) IN 1958 AND LEWIS R. HAGOOD IN 1965.

Extensive Expertise

Today, Hagood is the senior partner and serves on the management committee, together with Tom Scott, William Simms, Michael Fitzpatrick, and Rick Powers. Other attorneys at the firm include R. Kim Burnette, Keith Burroughs, Christopher Cain, Tom Cole, Steve Collins, Samuel Doak, Donald Farinato, Steve Hurdle, Gerard Jabaley, Arthur Jenkins, Carol Ann Lamons, Dan Rhea, Robert Townsend, and John Willis.

Every lawyer in the firm is expected to—and does—go to court.

"If you write a contract, you need to know how to defend it," Hagood says. "We're a litigation firm, as well as a partner to our clients in a variety of related services." The firm also has a strong presence in the fields of wills, trusts, and estates, as well as business and corporate transactional practice.

Most members of the firm are alumni of the University of Tennessee College of Law, where Collins currently serves as adjunct professor of law at the university, with several

of the other members of the firm having considerable experience as adjunct law teachers.

Integrity and Philosophy

Hagood attributes much of the firm's success to its two key areas of focus: the Four I's and a philosophy of preventive law. "When new associates join our firm, we always tell them to remember and honor the Four I's, which are integrity, intelligence, industry, and insight," Hagood explains. "Integrity is the most important characteristic of a good lawyer. There are no degrees of integrity, and you either have it or you don't."

At Arnett, Draper and Hagood, integrity is translated into serving client needs efficiently, economically, and ethically. Together with a philosophy of preventive law, these features have kept the firm's clients well served for some 50 years.

"We've had new clients tell us they previously never saw their lawyers until there was a problem," Hagood says. "We are proactive, and we devote serious time and effort to understand our client's business and its needs. That sets us apart."

The firm conducts numerous legal seminars for the bar association and national legal training

THE MANAGEMENT COMMITTEE SERVING THE FIRM CONSISTS OF (FRONT ROW, FROM LEFT) TOM SCOTT, SENIOR PARTNER LEWIS HAGOOD, WILLIAM SIMMS, (BACK ROW) MICHAEL FITZPATRICK, AND RICK POWERS.

organizations, as well as for its clients. "The homework required for our presentations keeps us up to date and better qualified to represent our clients," Hagood concludes.

Community Involvement

The attorneys at Arnett, Draper and Hagood give of their time and talent through pro bono work by representing individuals in selected legal cases, serving on the boards of numerous community organizations, and contributing both their time and money to such organizations.

"We are unified in thought on this issue," Scott says. "We earn our livelihood from the community of Knoxville, and we have all committed ourselves to giving something back to this special place."

Arnett, Draper, and Scott have all served as president of the Knoxville Bar Association, and are all members of the prestigious American College

of Trial Lawyers. Doak currently serves as president of the Knoxville Barristers, and Scott is the current president of the Knoxville Legal Aid Society. All members of the firm are active in the Tennessee Bar Association, and a number have served or are currently serving in various capacities. In addition, Arnett, who is now retired, has served as president of the Tennessee Bar Association and in important posts in many other legal organizations, as have a number of the other attorneys in the firm. Hagood is a member and secretary of the Tennessee Board of Law Examiners.

In addition to their work as advocates, a number of the firm's lawyers serve as mediators in many significant cases. Hagood and Powers are listed in The Best Lawyers in America, and, together with their partners and associates, are part of a firm that is highly regarded in the profession. With its principal focus on legal skill and integrity, Arnett, Draper and Hagood has proven itself over time as a true leader in the Knoxville area.

CLOCKWISE FROM TOP LEFT: IN ADDITION TO THEIR WORK AS ADVOCATES, A NUMBER OF THE FIRM'S LAWYERS SERVE AS MEDIATORS IN MANY SIGNIFICANT CASES. SHOWN ARE (FROM LEFT) LEWIS HAGOOD, STEVE COLLINS, TOM SCOTT, KEITH BURROUGHS, R. KIM BURNETTE, AND STEVE HURDLE.

ALL MEMBERS OF THE FIRM, INCLUDING (FROM LEFT) CHRISTOPHER CAIN, TOM COLE, DONALD FARINATO, JOHN WILLIS, CAROL ANN LAMONS, AND ARTHUR JENKINS, ARE ACTIVE IN THE TENNESSEE BAR ASSOCIATION.

JEAN THOMAS IS EXECUTIVE SECRETARY AND OFFICE MANAGER FOR THE FIRM.

OTHER MEMBERS OF THE FIRM INCLUDE (FROM LEFT) DAN RHEA, SAMUEL DOAK, AND ROBERT TOWNSEND.

The University of Tennessee Medical Center

A S A TEACHING HOSPITAL, THE UNIVERSITY OF TENNESSEE (UT) MEDICAL CENTER STANDS APART FROM ITS MEDICAL SERVICE COUNTERPARTS IN KNOXVILLE. "EVERY DAY, STUDENTS CHALLENGE ME WITH TOUGH QUESTIONS," EXPLAINS DR. DALE WORTHAM, CARDIOLOGIST. "BECAUSE I HAVE TO KNOW THE ANSWERS, I'M COMPELLED TO KEEP UP WITH THE LATEST RESEARCH AND MEDICAL BREAKTHROUGHS.

This challenging environment helps make me a better doctor, and that helps me give my patients the best care possible."

UT Medical Center includes UT Memorial Hospital and UT Graduate School of Medicine. The hospital was founded in 1956 with a threefold mission still in existence today: health care, medical education, and clinical research. Today, UT Medical Center serves 24 counties in East Tennessee, along with portions of western North Carolina, southwestern Virginia, and southeastern Kentucky.

Diverse Facilities

The hospital operates 581 acute care beds and a 21-bed skilled nursing facility that provides transitional care between a hospital and a nursing home stay. In 2000, the hospital recorded 21,232 inpatient admissions, 48,125 emergency room visits, and hundreds of thousands of outpatient visits.

As the primary teaching site for UT Graduate School of Medicine, UT Medical Center is one of only 450 teaching hospitals across the nation. In 1999, the hospital was recognized by HCIA and the Health Network as a recipient of the 100 Top Hospitals™ award in the major teaching hospitals category.

UT Graduate School of Medicine offers accredited residency programs in 10 disciplines: anesthesiology, family medicine, general surgery, internal medicine, nuclear medicine, obstetrics and gynecology, pathology, radiology, general dentistry, and oral and maxillofacial surgery. Fellowships are offered in sports medicine, vascular surgery, and trauma/critical care.

A wide range of services makes UT Medical Center unique to the East Tennessee area. The hospital is the region's only Level I pediatric and adult trauma center, which includes the Lifestar rapid air transport operation. The hospital has also been designated by the state to provide care to high-risk mothers and their infants: It serves as the region's Level III intensive care nursery, and provides the region's only pediatric open-heart surgery program.

In addition, UT Medical Center is the only hospital in the area that provides kidney transplants and stem cell transplants for oncology patients. The hospital was the first location in the country to offer positron emission tomography in a clinical setting, and is the site of the only clinical cyclotron in the region, which supplies radiopharmaceuticals.

Unique Services

Other special services at UT Medical Center are provided by the East Tennessee Hemophilia Center, Developmental and Genetic Center, and UT Home Care Services. The comprehensive health care system also includes numerous outpatient services and telemedicine technology. In addition, satellite offices are located for convenience in West Knoxville, Farragut, Tellico Village, Halls, Sevierville, and LaFollette.

Under the guidance of Mickey Bilbrey, CEO for University Health System, UT Medical Center continues to take steps to remain at the forefront of East Tennessee health care. The newly renovated trauma center and department of emergency medicine feature 50 beds for specialized care in critical resuscitation, emergent care, urgent care, and pediatrics, as well as a special area for trauma intensive care.

"We are dedicated to developing patient facilities that meet the needs of this rapidly growing population and the demands of those who wish to receive superior services from physicians associated with a teaching hospital," says Bilbrey.

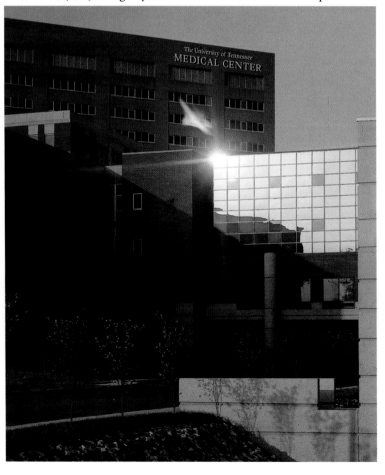

WITH A WIDE RANGE OF SERVICES, THE UNIVERSITY OF TENNESSEE MEDICAL CENTER IS UNIQUE TO THE EAST TENNESSEE AREA.

A S A TEENAGER IN 1968, MICHAEL STRICKLAND PROVIDED HIS FIRST LIGHTING SYSTEM FOR A TOURING ACT THAT STOPPED IN HIS NATIVE KINGSPORT. FOR $25, THE YOUNG STRICKLAND LIT THE SHOW IN THE HIGH SCHOOL'S NEWLY BUILT, 10,000-SEAT GYMNASIUM, THUS GIVING BIRTH TO BANDIT LITES, INC. TODAY, STRICKLAND IS CEO OF THE SECOND-LARGEST AND FASTEST-GROWING LIGHTING HIRE COMPANY IN

Bandit Lites, Inc.

the world. As Bandit Lites has grown from its infancy, so has its prestigious client list with names such as Garth Brooks, Jimmy Buffett, the World Wrestling Federation, Barry Manilow, and Lord of the Dance, to name a few.

Bandit gained its first major break and a solid foothold in the industry when it was named lighting contractor for Conway Twitty and Loretta Lynn. Bandit has been growing steadily ever since. From its world headquarters in Knoxville, the company operates seven offices worldwide, including production and design facilities in Knoxville, Nashville, and London, along with offices in San Francisco; Dublin, Ireland; Hong Kong; and Taiwan.

The essence of the business is to "paint the air with light and smoke," explains Strickland. The job of the lighting is to convey a mood and further enhance a performance. Bandit serves four major markets within the lighting industry: concerts and musical events; film and television; industrial, corporate, and trade show applications; and sales, service, and installations for new and existing facilities. "We are considered leaders in the concert and film-television markets, all of which represent considerable opportunity for growth," Strickland says. "We also see incredible potential for growth within the Asia-Pacific market within the next 10 years."

Company Standards

Strickland says that he and his management team have set high standards for every aspect of the company and its employees. Bandit is one of the few companies in the industry that maintains a completely full-time staff with full benefits from technicians through management. Strickland calls these aspects of company operations the Bandit Standard. Bandit Standards are a set of criteria meant to exceed customer expectations in all areas from design through installation of a project. National Sales Manager Jim Smerbeck explains, "When someone orders a system from Bandit, it is not a prefabricated package, but a tailor-made solution from the blueprints on." When an order is placed at Bandit, the system is completely built at the company's facilities, then tested and delivered to the client's venue.

Bandit Standards reach from the equipment provided to the quality of people Bandit hires. As a result of this commitment to quality, Bandit Lites has received numerous awards, such as Performance Lighting Company of the Year, Country Music Association Support Services Company of the Year, and Lighting Production Company of the Year in Europe. Business recognitions include the Ernst & Young Entrepreneur of the Year—which is sponsored by Nasdaq, CNN, and *USA Today*—and East Tennessee

Entrepreneurial Company of the Year, along with chamber of commerce awards in both Knoxville and Nashville.

A True Measure of Success

Strickland measures the company's success by the individual successes of its employees and their families. He believes in a philosophy he calls "humanomics," which combines the physical, economic, and spiritual aspects of each individual. Strickland believes in setting high personal goals for Bandit's employees, so that they see and reach their true potential both at work and at home. This philosophy can be seen through the company's many charitable contributions and outreach programs, particularly in arts education. Strickland explains, "Caring is tantamount to basic human well-being. If we care, everything turns out for the better. That is true with regard to our employees, as well as to our customers. As a result, our goals for the company fit into two categories: better service for clients and better living for the employees."

According to Strickland, Knoxville fits well into Bandit's future plans. He notes the city's high quality of life for employees and its low cost of doing business for customers. While other communities constantly court Bandit Lites from across the country, Strickland's wish is to remain in East Tennessee.

BANDIT LITES, INC. SERVES FOUR MAJOR MARKETS WITHIN THE LIGHTING INDUSTRY: CONCERTS AND MUSICAL EVENTS; FILM AND TELEVISION; INDUSTRIAL, CORPORATE, AND TRADE SHOW APPLICATIONS; AND SALES, SERVICE, AND INSTALLATIONS FOR NEW AND EXISTING FACILITIES.

Rice Automotive Group

N 1957, KEN RICE OPENED THE FIRST RICE AUTOMOTIVE DEALERSHIP ON CUMBERLAND AVENUE IN KNOXVILLE. WHAT BEGAN AS A SMALL DEALERSHIP HAS GROWN TO BECOME A SUCCESSFUL—AND SIZABLE—AUTOMOTIVE GROUP WITH A LOYAL CUSTOMER BASE AND SALES OF MORE THAN $60 MILLION IN 1999. THE GROWTH OF THE BUSINESS PROMPTED THE DEALERSHIP'S MOVE TO A 10-ACRE SITE ON KINGSTON PIKE NEAR BEARDEN HIGH SCHOOL IN 1971.

The Airport Motor Mile dealership, Rice Chrysler Plymouth Dodge, opened in 1985. Rice Automotive sells GMC trucks, as well as Oldsmobile, Mitsubishi, Chrysler, and Dodge vehicles. A full-service body shop is available, along with well-stocked used car lots at each location.

From the beginning, Rice Automotive has been a family-oriented business. Rice's sons-in-law, Don Campbell and Curtis Wright, joined the company in 1974 and 1979, respectively, and were both integral to the expansion efforts. Today, Campbell is in charge of the Kingston Pike dealership, while Wright manages the Alcoa Highway location. Recently, a third-generation family member joined Rice Automotive: Campbell's son, Scott, came on staff as sales manager in 1995.

"We're proud to be active, non-absentee owners," Don Campbell says. "We're a family business that cares about our employees and our customers. We're very different

from the megadealers increasingly common in the industry."

Service and Loyalty

Rice Automotive's success and longevity come from its intense emphasis on service, which leads to customer and employee loyalty. "We've been focused on superior service for more than 40 years," says Campbell, "and we try to make service as convenient as possible. Unless you provide excellent service, you won't see customers return again and again."

Rice Automotive service works to remain competitive in price with the mass-market service companies cropping up throughout the city. According to Campbell, customers sometimes have the misperception that dealership service has to be expensive. "That's just not true at Rice," he says, adding that all of the company's technicians are factory trained and have access to the most advanced computer systems for service.

In addition, of the 130 employees at the two dealerships, 39 have been with the company 10 or more years. "I think that says a lot," Campbell says. "We take care of our employees as well as our customers. Ultimately, the customers benefit the most because we have one of the most experienced staffs in the industry."

"It's all about relationships," says Wright. "People buy from people, especially if they're new to a dealership. I think the greatest accomplishments at Rice Automotive are the integrity and professionalism we've brought to the car business. It means we can be trusted, and trust is often hard to earn in this business."

Sales Consultant Gary Cox has sold cars for more than 40 years—he has even sold to three and four generations of the same families—making him one of six Rice Automotive Group employees who have worked 30 or more years for the company. "Rice provides an atmosphere that I like," Cox explains. "You have

RICE AUTOMOTIVE GROUP OPENED ITS FIRST DEALERSHIP IN 1957 AND HAS GROWN INTO A SUCCESSFUL—AND SIZABLE— GROUP WITH A LOYAL CUSTOMER BASE.

to love automobiles, both the engineering aspects and the physical driving aspects. I enjoy my time at Rice because many of the people I've met have become good friends over the years. Rice takes good care of its customers after the sale. It's a very nice working atmosphere here, like family."

Thriving on Industry Change

Both Campbell and Wright have witnessed dramatic changes in the automobile world over the past three decades. They cite the dominance of SUVs and minivans as two of the greatest trends to ever hit the industry; the vehicles account for nearly 50 percent of the company's business. In response to these trends, the company is constantly developing new systems to better manage customer relationships and to tap the strength of today's technology.

Rice Automotive's commitment to remaining on top of industry changes and trends has resulted in increased growth and success. "We now have such a wide variety of products, in a broad range of price points," Campbell says, noting Oldsmobile's evolution toward a younger market, with cars like the Oldsmobile Alero and Intrigue.

For Wright, one of the biggest changes in the industry has been the amount of information at the buyers'

fingertips. "Cars are more expensive and buyers are more sophisticated," he says. "They're armed with a lot more information, primarily from the Internet. They're less loyal to one particular brand, and more willing to simply buy what they like."

At the beginning of this new century, Rice Automotive Group stands ready with an enthusiastic commitment to professionalism and service. "As we address the future, we'll stay focused on service and continue to stay atop the constant change in this industry," Campbell says. "No matter what happens within the industry, though, people will always want to be dealt with one-on-one, with quality service and professionalism. That's what we deliver."

RICE AUTOMOTIVE'S SUCCESS AND LONGEVITY COME FROM ITS INTENSE EMPHASIS ON SERVICE, WHICH LEADS TO CUSTOMER AND EMPLOYEE LOYALTY.

Cherokee Distributing Company

NSCRIBED UPON A PODIUM IN THE CONFERENCE ROOM AT CHEROKEE DISTRIBUTING COMPANY IS THIS MOTTO: "A COMPANY IS KNOWN BY THE PEOPLE IT EMPLOYS." SINCE 1958, CHEROKEE DISTRIBUTING COMPANY HAS ADHERED TO THAT POLICY, MAKING EVERY EFFORT TO ATTRACT AND RETAIN GOOD EMPLOYEES. THAT APPROACH HAS PAID OFF IN THE FORM OF A WORKFORCE COMPOSED OF ENTHUSIASTIC AND DEDICATED INDIVIDUALS.

"This is a family business," says Nell Sampson, president of the company that was started by her father, George Sampson. "The gentlemen here are like my brothers." She notes that a team of approximately 80 employees work as drivers, superintendents, warehouse workers, and other support roles in the company, which distributes some 2.5 million cases of beer annually.

Miller Brewing Company

According to George Sampson, chairman and CEO of the company, the situation improved for Cherokee in 1971 when Philip Morris bought Miller Brewing Company. "The following year, Knoxville was selected as one of the first test markets for Miller Lite, and business really began expanding. By 1974, growing sales necessitated a move to a larger warehouse," says Sampson.

In the early days, Miller beer only came in one size: 12-ounce cans and bottles. Today, Miller products come in a variety of shapes and sizes. The Miller Brewing Company produces high-quality products from malted barley, select cereal grains, pure water, and choice hops. Cherokee carries the complete Miller line, which includes Miller High Life, Genuine Draft, Genuine Draft Light, Miller Lite, Lite Ice, Icehouse, Lowenbrau, Miller Reserve, Reserve Velvet Stout, and Reserve Amber Ale.

In 1981, Cherokee needed an even larger warehouse, so the company constructed a new facility. In response to a changing marketplace, the firm added import products, test-marketed new brands, initiated a recycled-can program, and incorporated computer technology. Cherokee also supports its customers with advertising, marketing, and merchandising programs, which help them sell more Miller

products. The company provides the heavily researched and computer-designed Spaceman merchandising arrangement system. "Our success is due to giving our retailers good service and to carrying a quality line of beer," says Sampson.

State-of-the-Art Facilities

The quality of our facilities and equipment complements the quality of our employees," Sampson says. The 127,775-square-foot facility includes 54,450 square feet of controlled environment warehouse areas; a 5,000-keg-capacity draft cooler; 30,000 square feet of enclosed drive-through and winter parking; a continuous dock that can accommodate nine railcars; and a 5,000-square-foot, enclosed truck maintenance and shop area.

From its corporate headquarters, Cherokee services approximately 1,500 customers throughout 15 East

KNOXVILLE HAS BEEN HOME TO CHEROKEE DISTRIBUTING COMPANY SINCE 1958.

Tennessee counties. Other amenities at the company's offices include a multimedia conference and employment development area that seats 100 people. In addition to the Knoxville location, Cherokee has ventured into Johnson City and Norfolk, Virginia, with new facilities.

Ron Buck works as general manager at the Knoxville location, overseeing the sales and distribution of products. He joined the company in 1974, when he was 18 years old, and says he has held practically every position in the organization, from route trainee to salesman, as well as supervisor, warehouse manager, operations manager, and sales manager. Buck is responsible for the company's 27 routes in Knoxville.

"This is a family-run business with owners who are present for advice and counsel," Buck says. "They're involved on a daily basis, and this is a great organization to work with."

Award-Winning Operations

Cherokee is one of only two all-time Miller Grand Master award recipients in the world. Additionally, the company has consistently won the Miller Masters Award, an honor bestowed on only 30 out of 700 distributors of Miller Brewing Company brands each year. The award recognizes Cherokee's stringent standards in every phase of the company's operation: sales, marketing, controls, fleet, image, and policy response.

In addition to being known as a leader in its industry, Cherokee is also known as a leader in its community. The locally grown company has a long history of giving back to the area via contributions and assistance to numerous civic organizations, including United Way, Big Brothers/ Big Sisters, St. Mary's Foundation, Knoxville Museum of Art, Knoxville Symphony, Knoxville Zoo, and Helen Ross McNabb Center.

"We have always been involved in the community," explains Nell Sampson. "The community supports us and our business, so we like to return the favor when and where we can. Cherokee Distributing Company has a strong presence throughout the East Tennessee region. We're known for our support of and participation in projects that help others."

THE SKY IS THE LIMIT FOR CHEROKEE DISTRIBUTING, A COMPANY THAT GIVES BACK TO ITS COMMUNITY BY SUPPORTING LOCAL ATTRACTIONS LIKE THE KNOXVILLE ZOO.

Hyatt Regency Knoxville

SINCE 1972, THE HYATT REGENCY KNOXVILLE HAS BEEN KNOWN AS THE CITY'S PREMIER FULL-SERVICE HOTEL. WITH ITS 385 LUXURIOUS GUEST ROOMS, THE HOTEL AND ITS COURTEOUS STAFF WELCOME BUSINESS TRAVELERS AND TOURISTS ALIKE WITH TOP-QUALITY FACILITIES AND ATTENTIVE SERVICE—WHAT THE STAFF CALLS THE HYATT TOUCH. "WE FOCUS ON BECOMING AS GOOD AS WE CAN BE AT WHAT WE DO," SAYS TOM MASON, GENERAL MANAGER.

THE HYATT REGENCY KNOXVILLE CURRENTLY FINDS ITSELF SURROUNDED BY THE NEW VOLUNTEER LANDING DEVELOPMENT WITH A GROUP OF ATTRACTIONS, EATERIES, AND ENTERTAINMENT OPTIONS FOR THE ENTIRE FAMILY (LEFT).

THE HYATT AND ITS COURTEOUS STAFF WELCOME BUSINESS TRAVELERS AND TOURISTS ALIKE WITH TOP-QUALITY FACILITIES AND ATTENTIVE SERVICE— WHAT THE STAFF CALLS THE HYATT TOUCH (RIGHT).

The hotel is the largest in the city. "We're set up to be all things to all people, whether business travelers or recreational travelers—people attending conventions and meetings, social catering events, or various day meetings," Mason says. "You can think of us as the venue for all of your travel and catering needs."

In addition to enjoying upscale amenities in guest rooms, including business and entertainment technology, leisure guests can catch a game on one of 24 televisions at Knuckles Sports Bar or enjoy casual dining at the Country Garden Restaurant. The Country Garden also offers a sumptuous Sunday buffet, rated one of the best in East Tennessee.

Meeting planners often turn to the Hyatt for its extensive facilities, which are unequaled in the city of Knoxville. The Regency Ballroom accommodates groups of approximately 1,000, an elegant boardroom seats 15, and a variety of additional rooms offer more than 20,000 square feet of meeting space. Exhibitions enjoy more than 22,000 square feet of display space and nearly 3,000 square feet of prefunction space.

Even More to Offer

The Hyatt currently finds itself surrounded by the new Volunteer Landing development with a group of attractions, eateries, and entertainment options for the entire family. The waterfront development includes the Women's Basketball Hall of Fame and the Gateway Regional Visitor Center, which includes state-of-the-art exhibits showcasing the region's national parks, cultural history, and technology marvels. Nearby are the James White Fort, Blount Mansion, Riverside Tavern by Regas, Calhoun's restaurant, Tennessee Grill restaurant, Volunteer Landing Marina, Star of Knoxville riverboat, and Three Rivers Rambler scenic railroad.

"We're so happy to see the downtown area around us develop so beautifully," says Mason. "For years, we have enjoyed our close proximity to downtown and the Civic Coliseum. Now we have even more to offer our guests."

Creating Loyal Customers

Mason says he's most proud of the fact that many of the Hyatt Regency Knoxville's guests come back again and again. From individual business travelers known on a first-name basis by the staff, to businesses and nonprofits across the East Tennessee region, to many education-related events, the list of repeat business is long. Such clients include Pilot Corporation, SeaRay Boats, the University of Tennessee, St. Mary's Medical Center, Baptist Health System, DeRoyal, Leadership Knoxville, and *The Knoxville News-Sentinel*'s annual Academic Achievers program. In addition, each year, the East Tennessee Children's Hospital holds a major benefit event with nearly 600 attendees and two stages in the Regency Ballroom.

"Our list of special events and special customers is very long, and we appreciate each and every one of them," Mason says. "From the Lady Vols' Salute to Excellence to the many events related to the Women's Basketball Hall of Fame and the Knoxville Art Museum, we're proud to host so many events that make Knoxville a truly unique place to live and visit."

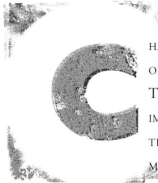

CHANGE IS GENERALLY CONSIDERED TO BE A NECESSARY PART OF AN ORGANIZATION'S GROWTH AND PROGRESS. SINCE 1979, THE TRANSITION TEAM HAS ASSISTED ORGANIZATIONS IN MANAGING CHANGE TO POSITIVELY IMPACT FINANCIAL RESULTS. ■ "COMPANIES CALL US WHEN THEY GO THROUGH MAJOR ORGANIZATIONAL CHANGES INVOLVING START-UPS, MERGERS, ACQUISITIONS, DOWNSIZINGS, AND WORKFORCE REALIGNMENTS,"

The Transition Team

says Donald R. Truza, CEO of The Transition Team. "We have developed processes that help companies protect their image and mitigate risk involved in such transitions. Drawing on our extensive experience working with Fortune 1000 companies, we design and implement programs to meet the unique needs of each client organization."

In start-up situations, for example, The Transition Team has served companies as the human resources department by hiring all the staff, leading the management team in developing mission and vision statements, writing employee handbooks, and advising regarding state and federal compliance. As the start-up company grows, The Transition Team can continue to be available full-time or to consult as needed.

The Transition Team companies also provide outplacement, retained search, loaned executives, leadership development, team building, executive coaching, project outsourcing, and a wide range of other human resource services. "No other company does what we do in combining this unique

group of services to provide solutions for our clients," asserts Truza.

A History of Helping Organizations Deal with Change

The Transition Team was founded in 1979 by Charles Pletcher, who started helping organizations deal with change as a speaker at Michigan's Oakland University. Truza became acquainted with Pletcher as a client, and opened the company's Knoxville office in 1992. Today, The Transition Team has an affiliation with more than 1,200 offices to meet the global needs of its clients. In 1998, Truza purchased the firm and designated Knoxville as its corporate headquarters.

Truza is certified as a Career Management Fellow (CMF) manager and a Senior Professional in Human Resources (SPHR). With 29 years of experience in plant, division, and corporate human resources with several international organizations, he is currently serving as the president for the North American chapter of the Association of Career Management

Consulting Firms International and was formerly the president of the local chapter of the Society for Human Resource Management. He is a graduate of the University of Akron and Kellogg's Advanced Management Program at Northwestern University.

Paul A. Ketchum and James B. Tait have joined The Transition Team as principals. Ketchum has nearly 20 years of experience working with small and medium-sized businesses, and Tait has more than 15 years of human resource experience with large multinational corporations.

The processes and practices developed by The Transition Team have led to a high level of client satisfaction as measured by the large number of repeat assignments. The Transition Team has received numerous quality awards from corporations and has been recognized by state governors, and its principals have been asked to speak at international conferences.

The Transition Team's goal is to be the premier provider of human resource services to companies undergoing transition.

THE TRANSITION TEAM PRINCIPALS (FROM LEFT) PAUL A. KETCHUM, DONALD R. TRUZA, AND JAMES B. TAIT BRING TOGETHER MORE THAN 65 YEARS OF EXPERIENCE.

Pellissippi State Technical Community College

ELLISSIPPI STATE TECHNICAL COMMUNITY COLLEGE OPENED ITS DOORS IN 1974 WITH ONLY 45 STUDENTS. TODAY, THE COLLEGE SERVES APPROXIMATELY 8,000 CREDIT AND 12,000 NONCREDIT STUDENTS EACH YEAR, MAKING IT THE SECOND-LARGEST HIGHER LEARNING INSTITUTION IN KNOXVILLE AND MORE THAN 20 SURROUNDING COUNTIES, AND ONE OF THE LARGEST COMMUNITY COLLEGES IN THE STATE. ■ ACCESSIBILITY HAS BEEN

"OUR MISSION IS TO BE A FULL PARTNER IN THE KNOXVILLE AREA'S ECONOMIC DEVELOPMENT BY BRINGING AN EXCELLENT EDUCATION WITHIN REACH OF EVERYONE WHO WANTS ONE," SAYS PELLISSIPPI STATE TECHNICAL COMMUNITY COLLEGE PRESIDENT ALLEN EDWARDS.

PELLISSIPPI STATE'S COURSE WORK STRIVES TO ACCURATELY REFLECT THE COMMUNITIES IT BENEFITS (RIGHT).

PELLISSIPPI STATE'S MIX OF COURSES IS CONSTANTLY CHANGING (LEFT).

the key to success at Pellissippi State, according to President Allen Edwards. "Our mission is to be a full partner in the Knoxville area's economic development by bringing an excellent education within reach of everyone who wants one," says Edwards. "To do that, we must continue to build relations with students, employers, and the community at large. We must expand our business partnerships, continuously update our curriculum, provide facilities that meet the demand for education services, stay on the cutting edge of technology, and ensure a top-notch faculty."

Convenient Campus Locations

At Pellissippi State, accessibility is measured in a number of ways. One of the primary measures is the convenience of the physical campuses. In addition to the main campus on Hardin Valley Road, just off Pellissippi Parkway, the college offers three additional sites. Located near downtown Knoxville, the Division Street facility delivers classes to urban residents and workers. And the Blount County campus has become so popular that a search is on for a larger location.

In 2000, a new campus on Magnolia Avenue in East Knoxville officially opened at the former Catholic High School location. This site will serve 1,000 students in an area that has traditionally had limited access to higher education.

Community-Based Education

Accessibility also refers to providing education for the entire community. Pellissippi State's course work strives to accurately reflect the communities it benefits. To serve the diverse population of East Tennessee, the institution offers a curriculum targeted to the needs of today's workforce. The mix of courses is always changing, and recent additions include classes on geographical information systems and e-commerce.

Since the majority of students are enrolled in college transfer/university parallel programs, Pellissippi State also provides program-specific articulation agreements with East Tennessee State University (ETSU), Johnson Bible College, Knoxville College, Lincoln Memorial University, Maryville College, Tennessee Technological University, Tusculum College, and the University of Tennessee. Through this arrangement, students can complete their first two years at Pellissippi State, followed by an additional two

years at the partnering institution.

In 2000, Pellissippi State expanded its agreement with ETSU in Johnson City for students interested in a four-year degree in engineering technology. Graduates of Pellissippi State with an associate's degree in civil, electrical, or mechanical engineering technology can now register and pay fees to ETSU, but take the remaining two years' course work at Pellissippi State.

In addition to college transfer, Pellissippi State also offers 20 career/technical programs designed for students whose primary educational goal is entry-level employment or career advancement. The overall job placement rate for 1999 career/technical graduates was 93 percent.

Pellissippi State goes beyond the classroom in providing an education. The community also benefits from a growing cultural program. In 1998, a full season of arts and entertainment was introduced, showcasing a diverse mixture of music, dance, theater, and festivities produced for the entire family. Each year, the program features talent of local, regional, and national acclaim.

Business Support Services

Pellissippi State is also accessible to business. The college's education and training efforts with business and industry were recently ranked as

the best in the state by the Tennessee Alliance for Continuing Higher Education.

As part of those efforts, Pellissippi State trained or consulted with more than 7,000 people affiliated with 165 businesses and industries in 1999. In a four-year period, the college developed more than 800 courses to meet the various needs of that niche locally.

Pellissippi State's Business and Community Services Division promotes the economic and community development of the region by providing high-value education in such areas as personal enrichment, advanced technology, business and professional development, computer training, contract industrial training, environmental and safety training, and quality and productivity. Joe Andrews, executive director of Business and Community Services, notes that during the 1990s, the number of participants in these noncredit

services increased from some 2,000 to nearly 30,000.

Pellissippi State also operates small-business development offices at the Knoxville Area Chamber Partnership, Blount County Chamber of Commerce, and Technology 2020 complex in Oak Ridge. These fully staffed offices provide classes and counseling to promote establishment, expansion, innovation, productivity, and management improvements of small business.

"I took the class on how to start a small business," says Gerry Harms, co-owner of the local Cedar Bluff Cycles. "It provided the groundwork for our whole business."

Massive Economic Benefit

When all of Pellissippi State's easily accessible programs are combined, they deliver tremendous economic advantages to East Tennessee. An economic impact

study was recently completed to measure exact numbers; the study found that Pellissippi State was a direct contributor to the economic vitality of Knox and Blount counties in excess of $406 million during the second half of the 1990s. That's an annual average of $81.2 million, $64 million of which is new, or external, dollars.

"It's significant that for every dollar of local revenues coming to Pellissippi State, there was $3.67 of local business volume generated," says Dr. Fred Martin, former vice president of economic and community development, commenting on the recent study. "Add in local income generated, and the total result is about $7.50 generated for every dollar of local investment. Of course, none of this measures the impact we have on the improved productivity and quality of life achieved through increased education."

CLOCKWISE FROM TOP LEFT:
AFTER OPENING ITS DOORS IN 1974 WITH ONLY 45 STUDENTS, PELLISSIPPI STATE NOW SERVES APPROXIMATELY 8,000 CREDIT AND 12,000 NONCREDIT STUDENTS EACH YEAR.

TO SERVE THE DIVERSE POPULATION OF EAST TENNESSEE, THE INSTITUTION OFFERS A CURRICULUM TARGETED TO THE NEEDS OF TODAY'S WORKFORCE.

IN ADDITION TO THE MAIN CAMPUS ON HARDIN VALLEY ROAD, THE COLLEGE OFFERS THREE ADDITIONAL SITES.

THE MAJORITY OF STUDENTS ARE ENROLLED IN COLLEGE TRANSFER/ UNIVERSITY PARALLEL PROGRAMS.

Knoxville Convention and Visitors Bureau

ARGETING MAINLY BUSINESSES AND CONVENTION ORGANIZERS, THE GOAL OF THE KNOXVILLE CONVENTION AND VISITORS BUREAU SINCE ITS FOUNDING IN 1979 HAS BEEN TO ENCOURAGE THOSE ORGANIZATIONS TO CONSIDER THE CITY AS THE PERFECT MEETING DESTINATION. TOURISTS, WHETHER BROUGHT TO THE AREA FOR BUSINESS OR PLEASURE, ARE A VITAL PART OF THE BUREAU'S CONSTITUENCY AS WELL.

Michael J. Carrier, president and CEO, describes his organization as a one-stop shop servicing tourism in Knoxville. One call to the convention and visitors bureau, and its sales staff will take it from there. "Every faculty member at the University of Tennessee, for example, is a member of some national or regional association," says Carrier. "We'd like to invite those associations to come here. That faculty member may not have the time or know-how to recruit that group, but we do."

Highlighting Knoxville's Assets

Carrier works with the 15-member Knox County Tourist Commission, a staff of 13, and many local volunteers to promote Knoxville. In the 1999-2000 fiscal year, the sales staff booked 45 meetings and conventions representing some 114,000 visitors. In total, these meetings were responsible for generating more than $103 million in total economic impact. Every year, the total tourism spending in Knox County is approximately $500 million, and contributes nearly $40 million in state and local taxes.

THE GATEWAY REGIONAL VISITOR CENTER, THE PRIMARY LOCATION FOR VISITOR INFORMATION ON KNOXVILLE, ALSO SERVES AS AN ORIENTATION AND LINK TO THE ENTIRE REGION AS IT CELEBRATES THE NATURAL DIVERSITY OF EAST TENNESSEE.

In addition, the Knoxville Convention and Visitors Bureau staff has worked with other organizations, pursuing the potential for an additional $260 million in total economic impact. The staff has attended nearly 20 trade shows to promote Knoxville, hosted 27 meeting planner site visits, and serviced 62 meetings and conventions that have come to town.

The bureau's communications department promotes the area by hosting travel writers, developing press kits, maintaining an updated Web site at www.knoxville.org, and increasing local awareness of the tourism industry. In the 1999-2000 fiscal year, these activities generated publicity in 41 publications, reaching more than 8.8 million readers.

"We have a great story to tell in Knoxville," Carrier says. "We are a tremendous destination for historical tourism. Not just our sites, such as the Blount Mansion and the James White Fort, but our strength in genealogy brings visitors to our area as well," he adds, referring to the genealogical center at the East Tennessee History Center.

Stepping Up the Competition

Whether promoting Knoxville as a destination for business meetings or family vacations, the Knoxville Convention and Visitors Bureau competes with cities throughout the Southeast. "Our facilities combine with our quality of life to help us attract visitors to the area," Carrier says. He lists amenities like the Knoxville Zoo, the Women's Basketball Hall of Fame, and the new waterfront development, Volunteer Landing, as popular places for tourists to visit.

"Our new convention center will allow us to compete on a whole new level," Carrier continues. "Instead of competing with cities like Johnson City and Kingsport, we'll be on the same level with Atlanta, Charlotte, Cincinnati, and other large cities. It will also allow us the opportunity to solicit meetings that have never been able to come here because our facilities weren't large enough."

The new convention center is expected to be completed in 2002. A total of 500,525 square feet will

be offered, with a 121,000-square-foot exhibit hall, a 30,000-square-foot ballroom, 26,000 square feet of divisible meeting space, and a 400-seat lecture hall.

"The biggest challenge is competing with these larger cities that often have promotional budgets as large as $20 million," Carrier says. "Our budget is less than $2 million. Working with our new advertising budget, we determined that people enjoy going places where they feel good. So we decided to get creative and present our area as a community that has fun with itself."

A considerable part of the promotional campaign focuses on the local community. "So many times, a community can't see the forest for the trees," Carrier says, noting that a recent public relations and advertising campaign targeting the local community won first place at a recent meeting of the International Association of Convention and Visitors Bureaus.

The ad's theme is "Think there's nothing to do in Knoxville?" and it goes on to list the many activities available. Carrier says the campaign will be repeated every spring to remind Knoxville citizens about the area's strengths as the tourist season kicks off with the Dogwood Arts Festival.

"One of our goals is to raise local pride," Carrier says. "We want people who live here to say, 'You ought to come to Knoxville and see what we've got,' because we're quite lucky to have a lot to offer to visitors, whether they're tourists on vacation or organizations looking for a great place to meet."

Grounded in its mission to raise awareness of Knoxville as a great convention destination and to attract both vacationers and visitors alike, the Knoxville Convention and Visitors Bureau is a valuable asset to the community.

THE OLD CITY HISTORIC DISTRICT SURROUNDS THE INTERSECTION OF JACKSON AVENUE AND CENTRAL STREET AT THE NORTH END OF THE DOWNTOWN DISTRICT. THE OLD CITY OFFERS VISITORS A UNIQUE SHOPPING AND DINING EXPERIENCE WITH A MIX OF ANTIQUE SHOPS, COFFEEHOUSES, RESTAURANTS, AND NIGHTSPOTS.

THE KNOXVILLE CONVENTION AND VISITORS BUREAU ATTRACTS VISITORS TO THE AREA, WHERE THEY CAN ENJOY SCENIC WALKS OR TAKE A CRUISE ALONG THE TRANQUIL TENNESSEE RIVER. VOLUNTEER LANDING INCLUDES THE GATEWAY REGIONAL VISITOR CENTER, ATTRACTIONS, RESTAURANTS, AND A RIVERSIDE PARK.

Knoxville

1980-2001

1980
Philips Consumer Electronics

1982
Hilton Knoxville

1982
Matsushita Electronic Components Corporation
of America

1983
Corporate Interiors

1985
Denark Construction, Inc.

1985
Gulf & Ohio Railways

1986
National Bank of Commerce

1986
The Trust Company of Knoxville

1989
Martin & Company Investment Counsel

1990
Kimberly-Clark Corporation

1994
Home & Garden Television

1995
Community Reuse Organization of East Tennessee

1997
Parkway Realty Services/First Tennessee Plaza

1998
Knoxville Area Chamber Partnership

1998
Marketing Dimensions

Philips Consumer Electronics

Tucked away on Knoxville's east side is an industry leader in television technology that has been there since 1980. With offices on Strawberry Plains Pike, Philips Consumer Electronics North America applies the latest in display technology to some of the most popular large-screen televisions on the market and is home to world-class customer support services. Outside Philips' main

entrance is a campus-like setting surrounded by the foothills of the Great Smoky Mountains, allowing nature and technology to meet at Philips' Knoxville offices.

For display technology, this Philips location designs, develops, and engineers large-screen projection televisions and television receivers for commercial applications. The company's team in Knoxville is a global product development center, designing products that are then manufactured in each region of the world. For example, projection television sets engineered in Knoxville are manufactured in North America, Europe, and Asia.

In addition, the firm's Knoxville site is the headquarters for Philips Service Solutions Group (PSSG), which provides extensive technical support, customer research, direct marketing customer service, and customer communication. PSSG offers consumer electronics and commercial equipment repair, hotel/motel electronic installation, factory-owned service centers, field-service operations, technical training, and award-winning service publications production.

PHILIPS CONSUMER ELECTRONICS NORTH AMERICA APPLIES THE LATEST IN DISPLAY TECHNOLOGY TO SOME OF THE MOST POPULAR LARGE-SCREEN TELEVISIONS ON THE MARKET AND IS HOME TO WORLD-CLASS CUSTOMER SUPPORT SERVICES.

Illuminating the World

Philips manufactures both analog and digital televisions, with features such as picture-in-picture, stereo sound, and special sharpness and clarity enhancements. Other Philips Consumer Electronics products include DVD players, portable audio, compact disc recorders, and computer monitors.

Consumer electronics represents only one of Royal Philips Electronics' many product lines. The $33.5 billion worldwide leader in electronics is also a leading supplier of lighting products, broadcast television systems, broadband network systems, medical imaging equipment, and a wide range of other products and services.

Established nationally more than 100 years ago as a lamp factory, Philips holds firmly to its roots and continues to illuminate the world. The company has lit such landmarks as the Eiffel Tower, Big Ben, the Great Sphinx, and Times Square.

With headquarters in Amsterdam, Philips employs a multinational workforce, with almost 240,000 employees working at 224 sites in some 60 countries. Known for its innovations, the company has recorded at least 120,000 inventions, 56,000

patent design rights, and almost 20,000 trademark registrations.

One in every two U.S. households owns at least one Philips product, and five of the world's top 10 PC manufacturers sell monitors produced by Philips. In addition, one in two telephones made in the world uses a Philips semiconductor chip. Each year, about 2.5 million heart procedures using X-ray equipment employ Philips' technology.

A Track Record of Community Involvement

The people of Philips Consumer Electronics have a long track record of community involvement, particularly with projects that involve children. A group of employees receives requests for support from the community and makes recommendations to management. Projects include United Way, as well as several youth- and sports-oriented organizations.

"Let's make things better" is Philips' company theme—both its rallying cry and its public commitment. "Let's make things better" can mean making better products, systems, and services. However, Philips attaches even more importance to making things better by contributing

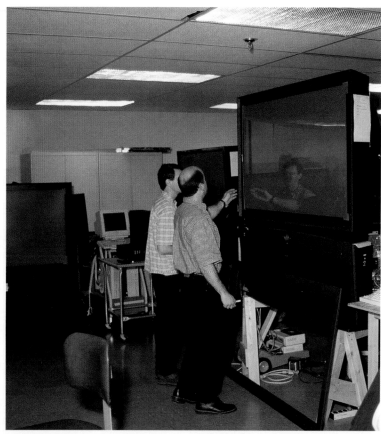

"In Knoxville, we have a talented, educated workforce you simply can't replace," a company spokesperson says. "We're able to attract people here because of the area's quality of life and low cost of living. We can entice people interested in leading-edge digital technology, and they can learn from very talented counterparts with years of experience in analog technology, all within a short driving distance of pristine forests or larger metropolitan centers."

Philips' employee population in Knoxville is comprised of diverse professionals who come from 23 states across the United States and nine foreign countries, and who contribute a variety of backgrounds and skills. The company's employees provide an exceptional level of dedication to Philips and its goals.

"The exciting thing about Philips in East Tennessee is that we have this huge organization, with the sharpest cutting-edge technology and tremendous resources, here in the foothills of the Smoky Mountains," management members say. "The most exciting applications in digital television and projection television are being created right here in East Tennessee." The combination of a great company, great people pursuing satisfying careers, and a great location all make the Philips experience in East Tennessee outstanding.

to improve the quality of people's work and lives.

For example, in 2000, in its capacity as a major sponsor of the Tennessee Smokies baseball team, Philips developed a unique way to raise money for the East Tennessee Children's Hospital. In its Strike Out for the Kids! program, every time a Smokies' pitcher strikes out an op- posing batter, Philips donates $5 to Children's Hospital. In its first year, this program raised more than $5,000.

Strong Knoxville Workforce

Philips employs approximately 400 people at its Knoxville location. People are why Philips has remained in East Tennessee, despite major corporate restructuring.

Hilton Knoxville

"**W**E KNOW WE'VE MADE A HIT WITH OUR CUSTOMERS WHEN THEY BOOK THEIR NEXT VISIT BEFORE THEY'VE EVEN CHECKED OUT," SAYS ROBERT W. KISKER, GENERAL MANAGER OF HILTON KNOXVILLE. REPEAT BUSINESS IS ONE WAY HE MEASURES SUCCESS. ANOTHER IS THE HOTEL'S OCCUPANCY RATE, WHICH HAS INCREASED SIGNIFICANTLY OVER THE PAST FEW YEARS SINCE IT OPENED IN 1982. ■ "BECAUSE OF OUR COMMITMENT TO QUALITY

and to doing whatever it takes, we have become one of the leaders in the market," Kisker says. "We have focused on building strong business relationships, invested in the property, and have become a significant part of the Knoxville community."

Southern Hospitality— Hilton Style

Located in the center of downtown Knoxville, Hilton has 317 spacious rooms that offer high-speed Internet connections and a long list of amenities. The Honors Floor also offers a state-of-the-art business center.

Guests have access to the hotel's outdoor swimming pool, sundeck, exercise room, and sauna, with beautiful views of the Smoky Mountains. In addition, guests have privileges at the YMCA across the street, which offers an indoor pool, racquetball courts, a jogging track, and a professional masseuse.

Standout Service

Kisker says that Hilton has developed strong recognition recently because of its warm and friendly service. A total of 130 associates are part of the team dedicated to delighting guests with hospitality and comfort, he says.

Many employees have been at the hotel for more than 10 years, including the chef, catering manager, and banquet manager. Jack's Steakhouse offers a casually elegant setting for breakfast, lunch, and dinner at the hotel, and the High Fives sports bar offers a fun place to unwind.

With the Hilton Knoxville's veteran team and 14,000 square feet of meeting spaces, the hotel features first-class convention facilities and services. The Hilton Boardroom is an ideal setting for a hospitality suite or corporate meeting, and the Cherokee Ballroom can accommodate groups as large as 700 people. A total of 14 rooms are available for

conventions and other meetings that require multiple spaces.

Kisker says his hotel is well known for its quality catering. "The finest people in catering stay here because of their strong work ethic and because they're working for a good company," he says.

"Our people are the key to our success," Kisker continues. "We're

all excited about the new convention center. It's sure to bring multiple opportunities, because we'll be one of the closest hotels to the new center. With our attention to details, our superb location, and the best employees in the city, the Hilton Knoxville is increasingly the first hotel that comes to mind with business travelers and meeting planners."

THE OCCUPANCY RATE FOR THE HILTON KNOXVILLE HAS INCREASED SIGNIFICANTLY SINCE IT OPENED IN 1982.

C ORPORATE INTERIORS CREATES ENVIRONMENTS THAT WORK. WHETHER DESIGNING INTERIORS TO CREATE THE PERFECT IMAGE OR TO ACCOMMODATE FUNCTIONAL NEEDS SUCH AS NEW TECHNOLOGY, CORPORATE INTERIORS DELIVERS DISTINCTIVE ENVIRONMENTS. ■ "WE OFFER A COMPLETE SET OF INTERIOR DESIGN SERVICES PLUS SERVICE AFTER THE SALE," SAYS SANDRA T. FITZGERALD, PRESIDENT. SHE DESCRIBES HER FIRM AS A FULL-SERVICE

interior design firm and office furniture company that specializes in planning, providing, and managing today's business environments.

Fitzgerald is a role model for women in business, having developed her business from a one-person shop in 1983 into a well-respected company with more than $8 million in revenues and about 30 employees.

A Design Team of Professionals

All of the members of the design staff at Corporate Interiors have obtained degrees in interior design, fostering a sense of professionalism among employees. What makes Corporate Interiors so effective, Fitzgerald says, is the team approach.

Corporate Interiors' specialists from the areas of design, sales, and operations come together to provide clients with quality products and individual service. This service comprises conceptual design, space planning, finish selection and color schemes, computer-aided design, furniture specifications, and project management.

The Corporate Interiors team coordinates planning, ordering, shipping, delivery, and installation of furnishings. Fitzgerald notes that Corporate Interiors' installers are full-time employees of the firm, which helps ensure quality control.

Creative Design Solutions

Corporate Interiors has successfully completed a wide range of multifaceted projects, including corporate offices, financial institutions, health care facilities, restaurants, retail establishments, hotels, and manufacturing facilities. Whether designing for a new building, a relocation, an upgrade in a current location, or a major change in configuration, Corporate Interiors delivers creative design solutions.

Among the company's recent projects are the Knoxville Utilities Board main offices in the recently renovated, historic Miller's building, as well as the new corporate headquarters for Clayton Homes. Corporate Interiors also works for some of the largest companies and governmental entities in the Knoxville area, providing ongoing service and daily support.

The interior design firm is aligned with two of the industry's largest and most reputable manufacturers. HON Industries and Knoll are both dedicated to the development of new solutions, quality products, and on-time deliveries.

Community Leadership

Fitzgerald is a native Knoxvillian, and a graduate of Central High School and the University of Tennessee. Fitzgerald's company is the only homegrown design firm in the area, and she is one of the few area design firm executives with a degree in interior design.

As a supporter of community efforts, Fitzgerald encourages her staff to participate in similar activities. She was part of the team that initiated the renovation of Knoxville's historic Southern Railway Station. Fitzgerald has served on the board of the Knoxville Chamber of Commerce and is a member of five

chambers of commerce. She serves on Knoxville's Workforce Development Board, and is active with the Nucleus Group, United Way, Shannondale Health Care Center, and other community organizations. Among Fitzgerald's past efforts are board positions with the Knoxville Museum of Art, Bijou Theater, Overlook Foundation, St. Mary's Advisory Board, and St. Mary's Health Dynamics.

"I'm one of this area's true advocates," Fitzgerald says. "This community has given so much to me, and I consider it a privilege to reciprocate by helping Knoxville and the surrounding areas that impact our region."

AMONG CORPORATE INTERIORS' RECENT PROJECTS ARE (TOP) OFFICES OF THE INTERNET PICTURES CORPORATION (IPIX), A LEADER IN DYNAMIC IMAGING, AS WELL AS (BELOW) THE KNOXVILLE UTILITIES BOARD MAIN OFFICES IN THE RECENTLY RENOVATED, HISTORIC MILLER'S BUILDING.

Matsushita Electronic Components Corporation of America

TUCKED AWAY IN KNOXVILLE'S FORKS OF THE RIVER INDUSTRIAL PARK IS A MAJOR FACILITY FOR ONE OF THE WORLD'S LARGEST COMPANIES. CONSISTENTLY RANKED AMONG THE TOP 25 COMPANIES IN THE WORLD, MATSUSHITA ELECTRONIC COMPONENTS CORPORATION OF AMERICA (ACOM) MAINTAINS ITS NORTH AMERICAN HEADQUARTERS AND THREE MANUFACTURING PLANTS IN EAST TENNESSEE. ■ THE KNOXVILLE LOCATION OPENED IN

1982 and serves as the North American headquarters for the electronic components subsidiary of Matsushita Electric Industrial Co., Ltd.—based in Osaka—and is an affiliate of Matsushita Electric Corporation of America in Secaucus, New Jersey. The ACOM group also includes divisions/manufacturing subsidiaries in San Diego/Tijuana and McAllen/Reynosa.

The Matsushita parent company, with annual sales approaching $70 billion, does business in more than 140 countries and has about 300,000 employees around the world. Its 14,000 electronic products are sold under the Panasonic, Quasar, Technics, and National labels.

Known to Most as Panasonic

ACOM's three Knoxville plants manufacture components under the trade name of Panasonic. Each plant's product is distinctive: aluminum electrolytic capacitors for electronic circuitry, processed aluminum foil for capacitors, and speakers for automobiles.

Customers for the automobile speakers include Ford, Toyota, Gen-

eral Motors, and Mercedes-Benz. Capacitor customers include Panasonic, Thomson, Sanyo, Ericsson, and Lucent; about 30 percent of the capacitor product line is exported to Europe and the Americas. About one quarter of foil production is used for ACOM's capacitor assembly operation, with the remainder exported to capacitor manufacturers on three continents or sold domestically.

Strong Growth in Knoxville

ACOM has the distinction of being the first Japanese company to locate in East Tennessee. The selection of Knox County was the result of a search for a centralized location that offered strong utilities, transportation, and human resource availability. The company's goal was to develop a North American manufacturing base in the highly competitive electronic components industry.

The plant opened with only two products—capacitors and speakers. Eventually, the facilities grew to cover three plants plus the ACOM group's headquarters. A single production building on the 40-acre site provides 370,000 square feet of floor space for 650 employees.

Continuous improvement—or *kaizen*, in Japanese—is essential to ongoing competitiveness. As a result,

ACOM applies extensive quality control tools, problem-solving techniques, and technology solutions throughout the organization. In addition, the company maintains an ever expanding training curriculum.

Most recently, ACOM has created the first manufacturing subzone to be affiliated with the foreign trade zone (FTZ) at McGhee Tyson Airport. By using the FTZ subzone, ACOM's Knoxville plants in many cases can import materials, assemble products, and ship them without paying duties on the materials. This allows the company to be more competitive on a global scale.

Binational Corporate Culture

ACOM's success and growth have resulted from creating a business culture that is founded in both Japanese manufacturing technology and East Tennessee practicality. The company has developed an organization and operating style that reflects its corporate motto: Communication, Cooperation, and Creation.

"The principles of the corporate motto are ingrained throughout every phase of company activity," says ACOM President Naoki "Nick" Kono. "We continue to find that our

successes are tied very closely to following the three Cs."

Special employee programs seek to go beyond breaching the language barrier. The programs invoke a spirit of cooperation and utilize team concepts in activities from the production floor to corporate recreational facilities.

By following the three Cs, Kono's company has received recognition made possible by aspiring to the highest international standards. ACOM is registered to QS-9000, the automotive quality management system standard, and to ISO 14001, the global standard for environmental management systems.

Local Youth Travel to Japan

ACOM is also building cultural bridges by sponsoring a program that takes four local high school students to Japan each summer. Since the first trip was made in 1990, the ACOM Tennessee-Japan Cultural Exchange Foundation has been established to continue the program in conjunction with the Knox County School system. The 12 local high schools can each nominate two students for this highly competitive program. The schools' nominations are based on academics, citizenship, service, interest in international affairs, an essay, and references.

Clark Brandon, assistant general manager, says the foundation pays all the costs for the four students and their chaperone to spend nearly two weeks in Japan. The students not only stay in Western and traditional Japanese hotels, but also spend a weekend in the homes of Osaka high school students. Brandon notes that several of the students who have participated in the exchange trip have gone on to develop careers in international business, and some have even returned to live in Japan. "We get postcards from around the world," Brandon says.

ACOM's community service involvement also includes an Adopt-A-School relationship with South-Doyle Middle School, support of United Way of Greater Knoxville, and miscellaneous Knoxville Area Chamber Partnership projects.

Blending Tennessee and Japan

The mission statement for Matsushita Electronic Components Corporation of America is "to manufacture items of good quality for daily use in abundant supply, thereby enriching and improving life for everyone." In the process of creating the very best electronic components possible, the company has created a working environment that blends the best of East Tennessee and Japan. Whether promoting better understanding through school exchange travel or through workplace programs, Matsushita has proved that blending American and Japanese cultures can be successful.

"We're developing a successful business that is truly an uncommon American enterprise," Kono says.

"We're cultivating an unmatched workforce through our motto of Communication, Cooperation, and Creation, and our continued success is proof that this unique blend of Japan and Tennessee works," says Kono.

CRITICAL DIMENSIONS ARE VERIFIED USING A COORDINATE MEASUREMENT MACHINE.

IN-CAR SIMULATIONS OF THE USER'S PERSPECTIVE ARE REALIZED BY THE USE OF A BINAURAL DUMMY HEAD.

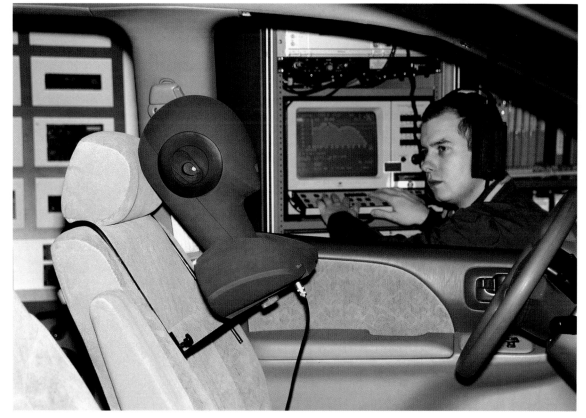

Denark Construction, Inc.

NNOVATION IS THE KEY TO SUCCESS AT DENARK CONSTRUCTION, INC. "OUR INNOVATION DIFFERENTIATES US FROM OTHER GENERAL CONTRACTORS IN THE REGION," SAYS RAJA JUBRAN, CHIEF EXECUTIVE OFFICER. ■ DENARK'S CORPORATE VISION IS TO BE THE PREMIER BUILDER OF CHOICE. "BY THAT, WE DON'T MEAN BEING THE LARGEST GENERAL CONTRACTING FIRM," SAYS FRANK ROTHERMEL, PRESIDENT.

BEGINNING IN THE SUMMER OF 2002, CONVENTION VISITORS TO KNOXVILLE WILL ENTER THE NEW 500,000-SQUARE-FOOT KNOXVILLE CONVENTION CENTER FACILITY, BUILT BY DENARK CONSTRUCTION, INC., THROUGH A SOARING, 78-FOOT-HIGH, GLASS-ENCLOSED ENTRANCE/REGISTRATION LOBBY (TOP).

THE WESTERN FACE OF THE CENTER OVERLOOKS A MAGNIFICENTLY REDESIGNED WORLD'S FAIR PARK—WITH CASCADING STREAMS AND LUSH NATIVE PLANTINGS—THROUGH A 400-FOOT-LONG, 48-FOOT-HIGH WALL OF WINDOWS. UNLIKE MOST URBAN CENTERS, THIS UNIQUE FACILITY HAS FOUR FACES TO BE CLAD IN STATELY BRICK, MARBLE, GLASS CURTAIN WALL, AND COPPER ROOFS (BOTTOM).

"Our goal is to be the firm that people think of first when they think of high quality, the smoothest process, and the best value."

Denark Construction, founded in Knoxville in 1985, enjoys more than $175 million of work in progress. Over the six-year period of 1994 to 2000, the company's operating revenues grew more than tenfold, earning it recognition as one of the 25 fastest-growing companies in East Tennessee.

Innovation in Construction

The company's innovation and teamwork have landed some high visibility projects, such as the Knoxville Convention Center, the Smokies Baseball Stadium, and the new headquarters/press facility for *The Knoxville-News Sentinel*. During construction of the stadium, Denark was faced with a schedule that competitors said was impossible to meet. However, the company's team of professionals not only met the schedule deadlines, but delivered the project two weeks early in order to be ready for opening day. By work-

ing closely with the owner and its design-build architects, Denark Construction beat the odds and completed the $13.2 million facility—with no change orders—in just a little over a year.

Construction innovations also helped Denark meet an aggressive schedule on the Maryville College Beason Residential Village. When rain threatened to delay the completion date past the start of the school year, the company devised a way to construct the roof while the walls were going up. A crane lifted the completed roof system into place and an otherwise-lost month was recaptured.

Innovations in Business

Throughout our history, Denark Construction has grown by seeking out the best people, the best delivery systems, and the best practices to ensure the best construction," says Jubran.

In addition to its construction concepts, the firm takes an innovative approach to business operations within the company. "Many times, people in the construction industry move up through the ranks without sufficient support," explains Gordon Knapp, chief operating officer. "At Denark Construction, we believe employees are our greatest assets, so we do things differently. We provide comprehensive benefits, professional training, and an open-book policy regarding corporate finances. We involve employees in our annual

business plan development. As a result, everyone is part of the team."

Innovations in Project Delivery

Denark Construction is the local leader in design-build, an approach to construction that is growing in popularity. With design-build, the owner, architect, and contractor work together from the beginning of a project to satisfy the owner's needs and budget. "Creating a team environment from the beginning is the best way to deliver value on a job, and to have it delivered on time and within budget," says Allan Cox, AIA, vice president, design-build. "Industry analysts say that most major buildings in the 21st century will use the design-build methodology, and that this method delivers projects 33 percent faster."

To improve the state-of-the-art in the industry, Denark Construction underwrites an annual symposium at the University of Tennessee. The symposium brings world-class speakers to Knoxville for area architects, engineers, contractors, students, and others responsible for contracting design and construction services.

Innovation in Philanthropy

We exist and are successful because of this community," notes Jubran. "The company contributes to our community because of this philosophy—a sense of obligation to give back." The list of nonprofit organizations the company supports through financial and volunteer contributions is a long one.

Denark Construction recently took a characteristically innovative approach to its tradition of philanthropy. When the company negotiated a contract to build the upper-bracket home of a local business leader, the owner and Jubran—two civic-minded executives—agreed on a very aggressive schedule with one condition: if the builder delivered on time, the owner would donate $50,000 to Denark's charities of choice. As a result of Denark's on-time completion, three local non-profits became beneficiaries of the client's donation.

With an innovative approach to operations, community involvement, and design-build construction, Denark Construction leads the way in its industry. "We have enthusiastically advocated innovation and collaboration," says Jubran. The results are technically superior, aesthetically pleasing, and economically feasible buildings throughout the Knoxville region, as well as a reputation for Denark Construction as an outstanding corporate citizen.

Gulf & Ohio Railways

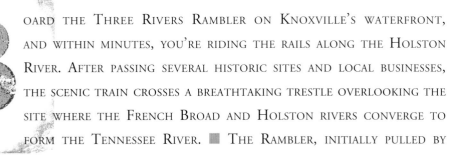

BOARD THE THREE RIVERS RAMBLER ON KNOXVILLE'S WATERFRONT, AND WITHIN MINUTES, YOU'RE RIDING THE RAILS ALONG THE HOLSTON RIVER. AFTER PASSING SEVERAL HISTORIC SITES AND LOCAL BUSINESSES, THE SCENIC TRAIN CROSSES A BREATHTAKING TRESTLE OVERLOOKING THE SITE WHERE THE FRENCH BROAD AND HOLSTON RIVERS CONVERGE TO FORM THE TENNESSEE RIVER. ■ THE RAMBLER, INITIALLY PULLED BY

two SW-1599 diesel engines, began operation in May 2000. In March 2001, a dream came true when a 1925 steam engine nicknamed Lindy was put back into service.

"I've wanted to operate a steam engine ever since I was little," says Pete Claussen, chairman and CEO of Gulf & Ohio Railways (G&O), operator of the Three Rivers Rambler. "Knoxville has had an ambitious waterfront project, and the Rambler should bring even more excitement to it."

The steam engine pulls several cars that have had distinctive experiences. The first-class car, called Resplendent, is a 1925 Pullman sleeper car from the Wheeling and Lake Erie Railroad. Two commuter cars, Trustworthy and Intrepid, are 1932 commuter cars that operated at Philadelphia. The open-air car, Dauntless, is a converted gondola, and the caboose, known as Desire, is available for charter service.

The Three Rivers Rambler departs Knoxville's waterfront park three times daily on weekends and holidays. The one-and-a-half-hour trip to and from the Forks of the River passes historic Island Home neighborhood, the Downtown Island Airport, several

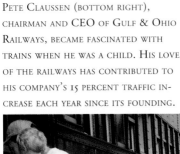

PETE CLAUSSEN (BOTTOM RIGHT), CHAIRMAN AND CEO OF GULF & OHIO RAILWAYS, BECAME FASCINATED WITH TRAINS WHEN HE WAS A CHILD. HIS LOVE OF THE RAILWAYS HAS CONTRIBUTED TO HIS COMPANY'S 15 PERCENT TRAFFIC IN-CREASE EACH YEAR SINCE ITS FOUNDING.

historic farms, the 1942 Mansion on the Hill, and a late-18th-century home at the site of the old Gilliam's Station.

Short-Line Operator

In addition to operating the Three Rivers Rambler, G&O also operates eight short-line railroads throughout the southeastern United States. The first line began operation in 1985.

The operation of short-line railroads is similar to that of commuter airlines, in that both transport cargo to and from customer locations for their larger counterparts. Throughout its system, G&O carries freight for Norfolk Southern, CSX Transportation, and Illinois Central Railroad.

In Knoxville, G&O serves major customers such as Ameristeel, Burkhart Enterprises, Rock-Tenn, and Tennessee Metals. Agricultural materials comprise a large portion of the freight.

Claussen notes that, nationwide, some 500 short-line railroads use approximately 50,000 miles of track, representing nearly 30 percent of the total route miles. "Hundreds of towns wouldn't have railroad service without the short lines," Claussen says.

G&O is headquartered in downtown Knoxville's L&N Station. In addition, the company operates the Knoxville Locomotive Works (KLW) at Coster Yard. The KLW facility rebuilds and repairs locomotives, railcars, and rail equipment. The site is also a switching area, where cars and cargo are transferred and dispatched.

Claussen, the man whose fascination with trains began as a child, has built a company that has experienced a 15 percent annual growth rate in traffic each year of its existence. He attributes Gulf & Ohio Railways' success to its people: "This company went from one railroad to eight in a little more than 10 years, and from eight employees to more than 80. But, not only did we get bigger, we got better. That's because our employees are second to none. Our safety record and reputation for reliability and quality exist because we employ good people, and they do their jobs well."

WHEN SHARON MILLER AND STEVE ARNETT DECIDED TO SET OUT ON THEIR OWN AND START THE TRUST COMPANY OF KNOXVILLE IN 1986, THE ISSUE WAS ONE OF CONTROLLING THEIR OWN DESTINY AND MAINTAINING A HIGH LEVEL OF QUALITY SERVICE IN MONEY MANAGEMENT FOR THEIR CLIENTS. TODAY, THE ISSUE IS ONE OF DELIVERING THE DESIRED LEVEL OF SERVICE TO THEIR GROWING LIST OF CLIENTS. THE COMPANY IS

The Trust Company of Knoxville

approaching $1 billion in assets under management and is the largest independent trust company in Knoxville.

Miller, president and CEO, explains that The Trust Company helps clients manage money and plan for the future by working to develop individual goals and objectives, and implementing investment plans. The company provides financial services for both businesses and individuals in areas ranging from estate to retirement planning.

"The Trust Company offers multiple investment disciplines, and the clients have the ability to set their own level of risk and control," reports Doug Bailey, a client of The Trust Company for three years. "The company works with successful money management firms around the country with a proven track record, and it provides readily available performance information in a format that can be easily compared."

A Unique Enterprise

Before they started their own company, Miller and Arnett worked together at Valley Fidelity Bank, primarily in the area of 401(k) plans. When corporate changes meant decisions were no longer being made locally, the two became entrepreneurs, establishing East Tennessee's first independent trust company, a state-chartered bank limited to trust powers.

"We wanted to have control over our own career paths and our ability to keep quality service," Miller explains. "We had grown accustomed to the high-touch feel of Valley Fidelity."

"Because of our ability to communicate and solve problems, our business has grown to approximately 50 percent 401(k) plans and 50 percent personal investments," Arnett adds.

Daniel Carter, trust officer, explains that communication is what sets The Trust Company apart from its peers. Since client objectives are

carefully established up front, he and the other trust officers have the authority to make immediate decisions on behalf of clients as situations change. "We have the authority to do whatever it takes to meet the clients' objectives," Carter says. "The standards of excellence are well understood here. We believe in disciplined, long-term investments. There was no panic here when the stock market dropped in

August 1998, because of our long-term, diversified portfolios."

These days, the company is enjoying steady growth, with new business generally arising from referrals from clients, peers, and friends. Miller explains that the some 35 employees keep their eyes on "being the best, not the biggest, and continuing to deliver the problem-solving client focus that has made The Trust Company a success."

THE TRUST COMPANY OF KNOXVILLE FOCUSES ON DELIVERING THE DESIRED LEVEL OF SERVICE TO ITS GROWING LIST OF CLIENTS.

SINCE CLIENT OBJECTIVES ARE CAREFULLY ESTABLISHED UP FRONT, THE TRUST OFFICERS HAVE THE AUTHORITY TO MAKE IMMEDIATE DECISIONS ON BEHALF OF CLIENTS AS SITUATIONS CHANGE.

National Bank of Commerce

N April 1873, the Bank of Commerce first opened its doors in Memphis. The cornerstone of its name, and the backbone of industry in the state, "Commerce" has stood the test of time. From the mighty Mississippi River to the picturesque Tennessee River, and now on to the great River Basin in North Carolina, National Commerce Bancorporation (NCBC), is a financial institution recognized and respected in the banking industry.

National Bank of Commerce, then known as NBC Knoxville Bank, officially began operations with a branch at the Kroger store on Chapman Highway in June 1986. Today, in this area, National Bank of Commerce employs approximately 120 people, while offering personal and commercial banking services to more than 20,000 households and businesses throughout East Tennessee. Major banking lines include commercial lending, automobile dealer financing, equipment leasing, private banking, nondeposit investment products, and merchant credit card services.

Conducting business with National Bank of Commerce is as close as the customer's phone or the Internet, at the touch of their fingers. Branches conveniently located in area Kroger stores are open until 7 p.m. weekdays and from 10 a.m. to 4 p.m. on Saturdays to coincide with contemporary lifestyles. Traditional branches located at Landmark Center, the Farragut Building on Gay Street, and the first freestanding branch at the corner of Kingston Pike and Durwood Road, offering drive-up banking and a night depository, reflect a more traditional bank atmosphere. Freestanding ATMs are also located throughout the Knoxville area.

"We emphasize quality customer service and provide intensive sales training for our employees," says Dan W. Hogan, president. "Decisions are made 'in market' to positively impact our clients. With today's lifestyles being as varied as they are, customers expect more from our employees. Our FSRs (financial services representatives) are trained to listen to our customers, identify their needs, and then provide the advice and the answers that will meet each customer's individual needs. Additionally, the purchase of Kenesaw Leasing and J&S Leasing, the two largest leasing companies in East Tennessee, has only strengthened the foundation of National Bank of Commerce in this area."

Revolutionary

Knoxville's National Bank of Commerce is part of NCBC, a regional banking organization that is the first financial institution in the nation to successfully employ in-store banking on a large-scale basis. After more than 100 years of successful banking in Memphis with a primary focus on commercial banking, NCBC opened its first supermarket branch in Germantown, Tennessee, in 1985. The idea was revolutionary, with customers receiving unprecedented convenience and the bank receiving tremendous efficiencies in operating costs.

Thomas M. Garrott, chairman of NCBC, was responsible for this revolutionary idea. A former wholesale food executive, Garrott noted the similarities between banking and supermarkets. They are both high-volume, transaction-oriented businesses where the velocity and turnover are more important than the margin. A symbiotic relationship now exists between NCBC and the Cincinnati-based Kroger Company.

Today, Kroger stores in Knox and surrounding counties enjoy the services of a National Bank of Commerce branch office or an ATM.

Growth Oriented

NCBC, the parent company of National Bank of Commerce Knoxville, can trace its roots back to that day in April 1873 when the Bank

NATIONAL BANK OF COMMERCE EMPLOYS APPROXIMATELY 120 PEOPLE, WHILE OFFERING PERSONAL AND COMMERCIAL BANKING SERVICES TO MORE THAN 20,000 HOUSEHOLDS AND BUSINESSES THROUGHOUT EAST TENNESSEE.

NBC'S MAJOR BANKING LINES INCLUDE COMMERCIAL LENDING, AUTOMOBILE DEALER FINANCING, EQUIPMENT LEASING, PRIVATE BANKING, NONDEPOSIT INVESTMENT PRODUCTS, AND MERCHANT CREDIT CARD SERVICES.

of Commerce opened its doors in Memphis, becoming the major source of financial support for the cotton industry. Today, the bank is still viewed as the primary "cotton bank" in the Mid-South.

NCBC delivers select financial and consulting services through a national network of banking affiliates and non-banking subsidiaries. Today, following its July 2000 merger of equals with CCB Financial of Durham, North Carolina, NCBC oversees $15 billion in assets and nearly 400 locations in nine southeastern states. The new company retains the name National Commerce Bancorporation.

"This transaction builds on the strengths of two successful companies," says Garrott. "Both companies are ranked by U.S. Banker magazine as being among the top 10 performing banks in the country. By combining both of our companies' core competencies and best practices, we can ensure that NCBC will maximize the financial product and cultural strengths of our attractive regional franchise."

"Delivering convenient and all-inclusive banking to our customers is our primary objective," says Hogan.

"Additional sites will be considered for future expansion, as the bank executes its hub-and-spoke branch banking concept. At National Bank of Commerce, we are focusing on our comprehensive delivery systems as we look to expand throughout East Tennessee. I believe we are positioned perfectly to acquire additional business. The future of National Bank of Commerce in Knoxville is promising, but challenging. As we enter the new century, the bank will continue to look for new growth opportunities and with that will come continued success."

NBC BRANCHES CONVENIENTLY LOCATED IN KNOXVILLE-AREA KROGER STORES ARE OPEN UNTIL 7 P.M. WEEKDAYS AND FROM 10 A.M. TO 4 P.M. ON SATURDAYS TO COINCIDE WITH CONTEMPORARY LIFESTYLES.

Martin & Company Investment Counsel

NTEGRITY, DISCIPLINE, AND CONSISTENCY ARE KEY WORDS AT MARTIN & COMPANY INVESTMENT COUNSEL, EAST TENNESSEE'S MOST PROMINENT INVESTMENT MANAGEMENT FIRM. REALIZING THE COMMUNITY'S NEED FOR INVESTMENT EXPERTISE WHILE SERVING AS TREASURER AND CHIEF INVESTMENT OFFICER AT THE UNIVERSITY OF TENNESSEE, A. DAVID MARTIN FOUNDED THE FIRM IN 1989. MARTIN & COMPANY INITIALLY MANAGED A TOTAL OF

MARTIN & COMPANY INVESTMENT COUNSEL MANAGES MORE THAN $1.7 BILLION FOR MORE THAN 150 CLIENTS. A. DAVID MARTIN (STANDING), TED L. FLICKINGER JR. (RIGHT), AND WILLIAM E. WOODSON JR. REVIEW A CLIENT REPORT (LEFT).

MARTIN & COMPANY'S STATE-OF-THE-ART TECHNOLOGY PROVIDES INSTANTANEOUS ACCESS TO AN ABUNDANCE OF FINANCIAL AND ECONOMIC INFORMATION. (SEATED, FROM LEFT) PORTFOLIO MANAGERS CHARLES STEWART, GARY HOEMANN, AND RALPH HERBERT, ALONG WITH DARREN WILLIAMS, JOEY BREWER, AND CHIEF FINANCIAL OFFICER DAVID JAGELS ANALYZE THE DAY'S STOCK MARKET ACTIVITIES (RIGHT).

$6 million for three clients; since then, assets under management have experienced steady and orderly growth for 42 consecutive quarters, even during periods of market downturns. Today, the firm manages more than $1.7 billion for more than 150 clients.

Martin & Company employs a staff of 16, including 10 investment professionals who bring more than 120 years of combined experience to their clients. Martin, who has received the professional designations of chartered financial analyst (CFA), certified public accountant, and certified cash manager, is president and chief investment officer. Martin directs the firm's overall investment philosophy and process. In addition, Ted L. Flickinger Jr., CFA, is executive vice president and portfolio manager, and is responsible for fixed income strategy. Also, William E. Woodson Jr. is executive vice president and chief legal officer, with responsibilities that include corporate strategy, business development, regulatory and legal issues, investment consultant relationships, and portfolio management.

Focused on Client Satisfaction

Martin & Company's select group of clients includes pension plans, profit sharing plans, endowments, insurance companies, public funds, financial institutions, trusts, corporations, and individuals. The minimum account size for new clients is $2.5 million.

"We have one business and one business only, and that is managing money on behalf of our clients," says Martin. "Our record of client retention is unsurpassed." He attributes this success to several factors, including superb service, a low client-to-portfolio-manager ratio, the latest technology, and highly qualified professional staff.

"Our greatest accomplishment is our client satisfaction," Woodson says. "Because of the limited number of clients we serve, we're able to spend a significant amount of time on every account. Our clients receive the attention they deserve."

In addition, technology enables the company to deliver investment management services comparable to those of the finest firms in the largest cities. "There was a time when you couldn't have a firm like this in Knoxville," Flickinger says. "However, our commitment to technology has empowered us. With our access to Bloomberg's financial service and other state-of-the-art technology for support systems, we don't take a backseat to anyone. We enjoy instant access to a wide range of financial information."

Dedicated to the Community

Although Martin & Company serves clients in 11 states, the majority of client relationships are centered in the East Tennessee area. "Our clients benefit by having us near," Martin says. "We're part of the community, and we're able to understand and respond to clients' individual needs."

The firm is also committed to community service, with employees serving on a number of community, civic, and nonprofit organizations, including the chamber of commerce, East Tennessee Foundation, Leadership Knoxville, Ronald McDonald House, Knoxville Museum of Art, United Way, and YMCA.

By dedicating itself to its clients and its community, Martin & Company Investment Counsel has established an influential presence locally, and will continue to deliver the highest-quality service in Knoxville for many years to come.

KIMBERLY-CLARK CORPORATION IS THE LEADING TISSUE MANUFACTURER IN THE WORLD, AND THE SECOND-LARGEST HOUSEHOLD AND PERSONAL CARE PRODUCTS COMPANY IN THE UNITED STATES. THE 128-YEAR-OLD CORPORATION'S WORLDWIDE TEAM CONSISTS OF 55,000 EMPLOYEES AND SALES IN 150 COUNTRIES. ▪ AMONG KIMBERLY-CLARK'S WELL-KNOWN CONSUMER PRODUCTS ARE

Kimberly-Clark Corporation

Huggies® diapers, Kleenex® facial tissue, Kotex® feminine care products, and Depend® and Poise® incontinence care products. The company is also a major producer of professional health care products, nonwoven materials, and technical and specialty papers.

In 1989, Kimberly-Clark chose Knoxville's Summit Tower as a base from which to centralize such functions as employee services, corporate transportation, and accounting and finance operations, which were previously spread across several locations. The Kimberly-Clark administrative center opened in Knoxville with three employees and has grown to accommodate some 400 people.

Neighborly in Knoxville

With such significant expansion, the center is soon to become one of downtown Knoxville's largest employers. And although Kimberly-Clark's administrative center is part of a $13 billion Fortune 500 company with operations in 40 countries, the Knoxville operation is small enough to stay focused on its role as a good corporate citizen.

The Kimberly-Clark administrative center gives back to the community through a long list of financial and volunteer service commitments. Its generous grant program benefits local nonprofit organizations, and its matching gifts program matches employee contributions to charitable organizations dollar for dollar.

Kimberly-Clark employees are active in United Way, the Adopt-A-School program, the downtown YMCA, and Knoxville's Promise. In addition, the administrative center assisted with the founding and organization of the downtown YMCA's corporate program, and received the Little Red Wagon Award as a Model Commitment Maker to Knoxville's Promise/The Alliance for Youth, part of the America's Promise program.

The company's commitment to Knoxville's Promise includes a financial contribution to the Schools of Promise effort, as well as employee volunteer mentors who work with Partners in Education, Knox County Schools, Vine Middle Magnet School, and Junior Achievement. In 1999, Kimberly-Clark employees mentored 600 students, nearly dou-

bling the company's original commitment. In addition, the administrative center loaned an employee for one year to serve as the pilot project manager for the AmeriCorps Promise Fellows program and Schools of Promise strategy.

In addition, Kimberly-Clark's good-neighbor policy bolstered the efforts of a local nonprofit organization to coordinate and build the Haley Heritage Community Playground in Morningside Park. A crew of 600 volunteers came together for a weekend to construct a community facility with 125 play stations. Today, the busy playground stands as a permanent testimony to a big corporation's small-town personality.

The company's community-minded efforts have not gone unnoticed. Kimberly-Clark has been included on *Fortune* magazine's list of most admired corporations since 1983. From its 1872 beginning in Neenah as a manufacturer of newsprint, to its current status as a worldwide consumer products company, Kimberly-Clark is proof that people are the most valuable assets of a successful company.

THE PEOPLE OF KIMBERLY-CLARK CORPORATION TAKE PRIDE IN MAKING PRODUCTS THAT MAKE A DIFFERENCE IN PEOPLE'S LIVES.

Home & Garden Television

HOME & GARDEN TELEVISION (HGTV) FOUNDER KEN LOWE SELECTED KNOXVILLE AS THE PERFECT COMMUNITY FOR HIS COMPANY'S HEADQUARTERS.

moving from city to city, building or repairing home after home, Lowe saw the need for television programming in these areas. While working as a broadcast executive for Scripps Howard in Cincinnati, he presented the idea to Scripps by drawing a house in which every room from attic to wine cellar was its own television show. To his surprise, the company loved the idea and agreed to invest $75 million.

As Lowe set about creating an infrastructure, he found his headquarters. "The lifestyle of the Knoxville community was a perfect fit," says Lowe. "I wanted a location where employees could have homes and families. The idea of the network is to inspire viewers to improve their quality of life. I wanted us to live like that." Describing the network, Lowe states, "HGTV is about how we live our lives—the hobbies we pursue and the places we spend our time."

Building a Successful Brand

HGTV is also about building a highly successful brand that resonates with viewers. On December 30, 1994, with 6.5 million homes in 44 markets, HGTV went on the air; five years later, the network had more than 10 times this number. HGTV's financial performance has been just as strong, with the network operating in the black after just four years on the air. The average cable network takes seven to 10 years to show a profit.

The prime-time lineup at HGTV's launch included more than 90 percent of original programming, a mix that quickly grew to 100 percent during prime-time. One of HGTV's original mandates was to own its own content. About 10 percent is produced in Knoxville; the rest is produced on location around the country and around the world.

HGTV discovered early on that how-to shows do not necessarily need celebrity hosts to attract viewers.

Viewer response proved that all that was needed were hosts who knew what they were talking about— someone to inform, inspire, and lead them to better buying and how-to decisions. Many of the original HGTV hosts are still on the air: Joe Ruggiero, Carol Duvall, Jennifer Convy, Kitty Bartholomew, Shari Hiller, and Matt Fox. In 1999, with the launch of the *Restore America* project, Bob Vila came on board.

Response has been overwhelming. Viewers keep saying they're addicted; from day one, they have been active participants. Initially, all questions and suggestions were handled by mail. Soon, HGTV began communications by phone and E-mail. Today, the program's Web site logs an average of 17 million page views a month from viewers looking for how-to instructions, new projects, on-line shopping, and live chats with experts and celebrities. *HGTV Ideas*, a bimonthly consumer magazine launched in 1996, provides program listings, tips, creative ideas, and new projects.

Expanding Programming

Realizing that lifestyle programming was larger than a single network, HGTV expanded its programming by developing other networks that appeal to viewers who are passionate about particular interests. In October 1997, when Scripps acquired controlling interest in Food Network, programming was energized and millions of dedicated viewers were added.

In September 1999, the Do It Yourself (DIY) network was launched. DIY provides simultaneous programming on air with on-line, step-by-step instructions and in-depth demonstrations and tips. The network combines new, original programming with material from HGTV's vast library. DIY fully integrates the power of the Internet: After viewing projects on DIY, viewers may go to the

IN OCTOBER 1999, HGTV CELEBRATED THE OPENING OF A NEW, $12 MILLION FACILITY ADDITION THAT DOUBLED THE SIZE OF THE PREVIOUS HEADQUARTERS.

DIYnet.com Web site for clear, printable instructions, plans, material lists, and more.

Scripps' youngest Web-driven network, Fine Living—launched in 2001—takes interactivity to the next level. Fine Living is an upscale lifestyle network that is a trusted source of information for those seeking the best quality experiences from around the world. The network covers the best of the best, from gourmet restaurants, luxury cars, and beautiful homes to investments, technology, and vacation experiences. The Fine Living Web site will function as an on-line concierge service that helps visitors find anything from the best home electronics to the longest-lasting roses.

In October 1999, HGTV celebrated the opening of a new, $12 million facility addition that doubled the size of the previous headquarters. In October 2000, ground was broken for another addition of 42,000 square feet. The current, 141,000-square-foot space houses some 550 part-time and full-time employees.

Not only is HGTV's West Knoxville facility one of East Tennessee's most striking, but it is also highly functional, utilizing the latest in computer graphics, video production, and Internet technologies. The facility is an all-encompassing home for E.W. Scripps' technical infrastructure; associates, such as Scripps Productions; and Scripps Networks, consisting of HGTV, DIY, and broadcast operations for the Food Network. Its Web-hosting area serves some 50 million Web page views a month from some 2 million content pages.

In downtown Knoxville, the E.W. Scripps Web-hosting facility at Digital Crossing incorporates the latest electronic advances. Located in the hub of downtown's high-tech redevelopment, the office hosts more than 1,200 Web sites and includes electronic storage for nearly 20,000 hours of content.

"We're embracing the future from a technology standpoint," says Lowe.

"HGTV is one of the most technically advanced cable networks out there. These advances in technology will continue to present opportunities for our viewers to experience and use our content in new and more innovative ways. Developments in video-on-demand, broadband, and wireless will enable our future to be both exciting and promising, while we remain true to our original mission: offer high-quality content that offers ideas, information, and inspiration."

NOT ONLY IS HGTV'S WEST KNOXVILLE FACILITY ONE OF EAST TENNESSEE'S MOST STRIKING, BUT IT IS ALSO HIGHLY FUNCTIONAL, UTILIZING THE LATEST IN COMPUTER GRAPHICS, VIDEO PRODUCTION, AND INTERNET TECHNOLOGIES.

Community Reuse Organization of East Tennessee

N THE 1940S, THE FEDERAL GOVERNMENT MADE A SIGNIFICANT INVESTMENT IN EAST TENNESSEE. THE MANHATTAN PROJECT ENSURED THAT THE UNITED STATES WON THE WAR OF ALL WARS, AND IT BROUGHT UNSURPASSED FACILITIES AND TECHNOLOGIES TO OAK RIDGE. TODAY, IN THE POST-COLD WAR ERA AND THE AGE OF GOVERNMENTAL DOWNSIZING, MANY OF THESE RESOURCES ARE BEING MADE AVAILABLE TO THE PRIVATE SECTOR.

This reuse, otherwise known as reindustrialization, is having a major impact on East Tennessee. From the reuse of machinery and buildings to the rebirth of a railroad, the Community Reuse Organization of East Tennessee (CROET) has been breathing new life into resources originally developed by the government.

CROET manages two unique properties, located in the East Tennessee Technology Park (ETTP), that are the prime resources for Oak Ridge economic development efforts. Heritage Center, previously known as K-25, currently offers nearly 500 acres and 850,000 square feet under roof. Horizon Center is a premier business park completed in October 2000.

Heritage Center

More than 30 companies are located in Heritage Center. Lease structures generally offer financial advantages to businesses willing to contribute to the facility's cleanup. In addition, tenants have access to some of the country's most advanced technologies and desirable equipment. Buildings range in size from 2,500 square feet to 450,000 square feet.

Heritage Center also offers amenities found at most high-quality industrial parks: well-established infrastructure; ready utilities; easy transportation via

interstate highway, rail, or barge; and professional property management. Differentiating services include unsurpassed security, strategic partnerships, and an extensive support network. In 2002, a new facility—measuring 66 acres under roof and with 75-foot-high ceilings—will be added to the inventory.

Horizon Center

Even before ETTP opened, the new industrial park was able to welcome its anchor tenant. Theragenics Corp.—developer of a leading-edge cancer-fighting technology—began constructing its $25 million, 100,000-square-foot headquarters in 1999. ETTP gave the company access to related technology, along with a convenient location and a capable workforce.

Horizon Center is a 1,000-acre Department of Energy tract of land on Oak Ridge Turnpike that has been turned into an environmentally oriented business park. More than half of Horizon Center will remain in a natural setting, with trails along Poplar Creek and special bridges to protect the area's watershed. The other half offers building sites that range in size from 10 to

100 acres. Visual aesthetics are ensured by covenant restrictions and public spaces throughout the park.

Successful Reindustrialization

With a total of $53.3 million committed to the region, and some 4,331 jobs created or retained, CROET is celebrating extraordinary results. Working closely with the Department of Energy, CROET is making sure the government's investment in this region benefits the people of the region for many decades to come.

"Reindustrialization is really having a positive impact on the lives of East Tennesseans who have jobs in the East Tennessee Technology Park," says Lawrence Young, president and CEO of CROET. "Thousands of families are reaping the benefits of reusing government facilities in Oak Ridge, as smart businesses turn to Heritage Center and Horizon Center to meet their specific site location needs."

Focusing on appropriate use of government resources in the interest of reindustrialization, CROET is proving to be a boon to area businesses and residents alike.

PARKWAY REALTY SERVICES IS GAINING A WIDESPREAD REPUTATION FOR ITS HIGH-QUALITY SERVICE TO KNOXVILLE'S REAL ESTATE INDUSTRY. THE COMPANY, WHICH OPENED ITS KNOXVILLE OFFICE IN 1997, IS A DIVISION OF PARKWAY PROPERTIES, A REAL ESTATE INVESTMENT TRUST THAT OWNS AND MANAGES OFFICE BUILDINGS AND OFFERS REAL ESTATE SERVICES TO THE REAL ESTATE INDUSTRY. ■ REFLECTING THE COMPANY'S DEEP-ROOTED

Parkway Realty Services

commitment to excellence in service and customer satisfaction, Parkway Realty Services offers a unique 4-F program. All of its buildings feature fresh flowers throughout, flags, fixtures that provide quality aesthetics, and fellowship through networking opportunities via monthly events for customers. Special coffees, University of Tennessee pep rallies, entertainment, and customer parties add a sense of community to Parkway buildings. In addition, charity theme events support local causes like the Angel Tree, Race for the Cure, Second Harvest Food Bank, and Knox Area Rescue Ministries.

"We're particularly successful in customer retention," says Matthew B. Fentress, regional manager, noting that the company's overall occupancy rate hovers around 97 percent. "We find that our customers like the services we offer so much that they tend to stay—at rates 20 percent above the national industry average. We're successful because we do thoughtful things for our customers without being asked to do so. That's just a reflection of our company's deep-rooted culture that places the customer first."

First Tennessee Plaza

The crown jewel of Parkway Realty Services in Knoxville is First Tennessee Plaza, the downtown office building marketed as Knoxville's symbol of prominence and prestige. First Tennessee Plaza is home to Club LeConte, a private dining club located on the building's 27th floor. In addition, a thriving retail area includes several restaurants, a gift shop, a travel agency, a dry cleaners, a shoe shine and repair shop, a newsstand, First Tennessee Bank, a copy center, a health club, and a FedEx office. The building also offers 24-hour, on-site guard service.

First Tennessee Plaza is Knoxville's largest, tallest multi-tenant office building, offering breathtaking

views of the Smoky Mountains, the Tennessee River, the University of Tennessee, and downtown Knoxville. The office building offers easy parking access and is adjacent to the City County Building and the Howard Baker Jr. U.S. Courthouse. A wide range of office space is available— from small spaces measuring about 300 square feet to entire floors measuring some 15,000 square feet.

Parkway Properties

Parkway Properties, headquartered in Jackson, Mississippi, specializes in the operation, leasing, management, acquisition, and financing of office properties in the southeastern United States and Texas. In December 2000, the company owned or had an interest in 52 office properties located in 12 states with approximately 7.4 million square feet of leasable space.

In Knoxville, Parkway employs 12 people and owns two buildings: First Tennessee Plaza and Cedar Ridge at Cedar Bluff Office Park. Fentress notes that Parkway Properties is involved mainly with premier, Class A office buildings.

In addition to leasing space in premium buildings, Fentress says that Parkway Realty Services is known throughout the city for providing high-quality service to building owners. This includes third-party leasing and management of build-

ings, as well as comprehensive real estate services.

"We have a very successful history of leasing office space here in Knoxville and across the country," Fentress says. With such a commitment to offering quality services and satisfying customers, it's no wonder that Parkway Realty Services is such a prominent force in the industry.

PARKWAY REALTY SERVICES' CROWN JEWEL IN KNOXVILLE IS FIRST TENNESSEE PLAZA, WHICH IS HOME TO CLUB LECONTE, A PRIVATE DINING CLUB, LOCATED ON THE BUILDING'S 27TH FLOOR.

A DIVISION OF PARKWAY PROPERTIES, PARKWAY REALTY SERVICES IS GAINING A WIDESPREAD REPUTATION FOR ITS HIGH-QUALITY SERVICE TO KNOXVILLE'S REAL ESTATE INDUSTRY.

Knoxville Area Chamber Partnership

WHEN KNOXVILLE AREA CHAMBER PARTNERSHIP PRESIDENT AND CEO TOM INGRAM CALLS THE PARTNERSHIP "YOUR CHAMBER AND MORE," HE MEANS IT. THE PARTNERSHIP, WHICH WAS ESTABLISHED IN 1998, HOUSES THE CHAMBER OF COMMERCE, CENTRAL BUSINESS IMPROVEMENT DISTRICT, DEVELOPMENT CORPORATION OF KNOX COUNTY, KNOXVILLE CONVENTION AND VISITORS BUREAU, TENNESSEE SMALL

Business Development Center, Tennessee Minority Supplier Development Council, East Tennessee Film Commission, and U.S. Department of Commerce Export Assistance Center and International Trade Center.

"Our goal is to make Knoxville as great a place to do business as it is to live," says Ingram. "If we can accomplish that, we'll have no competition."

Partnership Defined

Ingram notes that collecting the partner organizations under one roof represents merely the first step toward a larger goal for the Partnership and the community. "We want to be prepared for any issue at any given time," he asserts. "We exist collectively to support our business community and to contribute all we can to strengthening the overall economic well-being of this region."

Each of the various partners has specific responsibilities that it must work toward. The Chamber of Commerce works tirelessly to support existing businesses, encourage new

NATIONALLY PROMINENT SPEAKERS BRING NEW INFORMATION AND INSIGHT TO THE KNOXVILLE AREA CHAMBER PARTNERSHIP MEMBERS.

THE PARTNERSHIP SUPPORTS THE GROWTH, EXPANSION, AND RETENTION OF BUSINESSES THROUGHOUT THE REGION.

business development, and recruit new businesses to the region.

The Central Business Improvement District is a geographically defined district of downtown Knoxville. Working with its own board of directors and standing committees, the Central Business Improvement District works to assure that the city is a safe and attractive place to live, work, and play.

The Development Corporation of Knox County owns more than 1,500 acres of business and office parks in Knox County. The organization assists companies in assembling sites, developing buildings, assessing infrastructure needs, and promoting available incentives.

The Knoxville Convention and Visitors Bureau markets Knoxville as a year-round destination for travel. Target audiences include individual leisure travelers, group leisure travelers, travel writers, and attendees of conventions, meetings, and trade shows.

The Tennessee Small Business Development Center provides assistance to small-business owners and those who want to start their own businesses. Counseling and resources are provided by the Small Business Development Center at no cost to the client.

The Tennessee Minority Supplier Development Council works to build business partnerships between minority businesses who are suppliers and major corporations who are purchasers of these supplies.

The East Tennessee Film Commission works to promote the production of film, tape, television programming, music, and interactive media in the region.

The U.S. Department of Commerce office provides a full range

THE PARTNERSHIP OPENED ITS DOORS IN 1998, BRINGING TOGETHER THE REGION'S KEY ECONOMIC DEVELOPMENT ORGANIZATIONS.

of assistance to companies as they develop or advance business in foreign markets.

Partnership as Facilitator

Ingram explains the Partnership's role in bringing people together to make the business environment better. "These organizations bring the best team of people together to enhance the business environment," he says. "What the Partnership does is bring people to the table. The community's chances for success increase dramatically when the various parties come together. Our main role is to function as a facilitator."

Ingram cites several recent announcements that represent the fruits of the Partnership's labor. "Continental Airlines' maintenance facility at McGhee Tyson Airport became a reality because as many as 12 organizations worked together to make it happen," he says. The facility represents a $10 million capital investment to the area—the result of a joint effort—as does the new Digital Crossing high-technology business center in downtown Knoxville.

At the end of 2000, more than 25,000 businesses were located in Knoxville. The Knoxville Area Chamber Partnership worked to support them and approximately 2,000 members of the Chamber of Commerce with programs like the regional legislative agenda, the new Manufacturing Leadership Council, and

the annual Business Showcase with its attendance of some 3,500 people.

Partnership as Regional Player

By taking a regional approach, we increase our success rate even further," Ingram says. He notes the many resources within the region that make regionalism a natural occurrence in East Tennessee. These include the Great Smoky Mountains National Park, University of Tennessee, Tennessee Valley Authority, and Oak Ridge National Laboratory. Ingram calls attention to 16 institutions of higher education that are located within a 45-minute radius of downtown Knoxville, and notes

that workforce development partnerships are growing rapidly to prepare a strong workforce for tomorrow.

"If we become a well-coordinated, regional community; if we become a business-friendly community; and if we become a community that does a great job of selling our assets to businesses—all the while protecting the things that are special about Knoxville and East Tennessee—then we can have as much business as we want," Ingram says with confidence. "Then we will have plenty of opportunities for when we want to change jobs, for our children and college graduates, and for people with the many diverse backgrounds that make up Knoxville."

MEMBERS DEVELOP NEW CONTACTS AND STRONG RELATIONSHIPS AT VARIOUS PARTNERSHIP EVENTS.

Marketing Dimensions

CREATIVITY WITH A UNIQUE TWIST IS THE EXPERTISE OFFERED BY MARKETING DIMENSIONS, A MARKETING CONSULTING FIRM ESTABLISHED IN 1998. OWNED AND OPERATED BY ALEEX CONNER, MARKETING DIMENSIONS SPECIALIZES IN THE DEVELOPMENT OF PROFESSIONAL MULTILEVEL MARKETING STRATEGIES, ADVERTISING CAMPAIGNS, AND PROMOTIONAL EFFORTS, AS WELL AS THE DESIGN/PRINTING of publications, for both small and large businesses.

Conner notes that the term "marketing" encompasses a broad spectrum of components, including published materials to promote a product or service; market research to create advertising campaigns that successfully reach the right audience; Web site development/e-commerce with a business-oriented approach; media publicity for new programs/services; and customer/employee appreciation programs.

Addressing Client Needs

Believing that creating a unique marketing approach is essential to generating new business, Conner uses unusual approaches that appeal to specific demographic groups. "As one of the initial steps with a new client, Marketing Dimensions works with the client to develop a marketing plan with realistic budget expecta-tions, targeting new customer acqui-sition to increase a company's revenue potential," Conner says. Clients also find that having a formalized market-ing plan in place helps them stay on track in achieving their corporate goals.

Marketing Dimensions offers a comprehensive scope of services in the development of published materi-als, whether for direct distribution to customers or as effective promotional tools for the sales staff. "How a busi-ness presents itself to its audience is a crucial aspect of marketing," Conner says, noting her expertise in develop-ing creative concepts, text, graphic design, corporate logos, and print production.

"Another key to effective market-ing is securing visibility for the busi-ness in as many ways as possible," Conner says. "Marketing Dimensions has a very successful track record in working with press contacts, on both a local and a regional basis. Publicity in newspapers, television, and radio vehicles is an important facet of a good communications strategy, and it increases the number of times the targeted audience is exposed to a product or service."

While increasing new business is always a top priority, Conner advises her clients to make sure they continu-ally court their existing customers, due to the extremely competitive market climate. Strategies may include incen-tive promotions for referrals or special recognition programs for large-volume customers.

Impacting Attitudes

Employee appreciation efforts are also essential to maintain an upbeat, positive attitude within the business," Conner says. "Creating excitement about the product or service from an internal standpoint also enhances success from an external standpoint."

Establishing tracking mechanisms that accurately measure the effective-ness of promotional efforts is another essential component of successful marketing, according to Conner. These measurements can be an im-portant reference for the next bud-geting process.

A new service provided by Mar-keting Dimensions offers an artistic flair. Conner is also an impressionist artist with an impressive portfolio of oil paintings. This artwork is used by businesses as part of their corporate interior design, customized client cor-respondence, and corporate gift items.

Says Conner, "With more than 18 years of experience in marketing, my expertise is in providing added value to my clients with professional assis-tance to guide them in the right stra-tegic direction for achieving their business goals." With a firm footing in the industry and an innovative approach to marketing, Conner will surely lead Marketing Dimensions to new levels of success in the years to come.

OWNED AND OPERATED BY ALEEX CONNER, MARKETING DIMENSIONS OFFERS CREATIVITY WITH A UNIQUE TWIST (LEFT).

ORIGINAL OIL PAINTINGS, SUCH AS *ROSE CASCADES OF GIVERNY*, PAINTED BY CONNER IN FRANCE, ARE USED BY BUSI-NESSES AS PART OF THEIR CORPORATE INTERIOR DESIGN (RIGHT).

Towery Publishing, Inc.

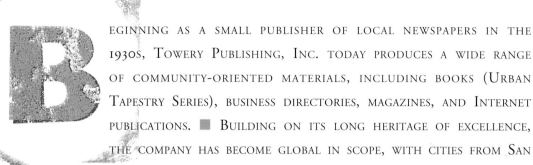

EGINNING AS A SMALL PUBLISHER OF LOCAL NEWSPAPERS IN THE 1930S, TOWERY PUBLISHING, INC. TODAY PRODUCES A WIDE RANGE OF COMMUNITY-ORIENTED MATERIALS, INCLUDING BOOKS (URBAN TAPESTRY SERIES), BUSINESS DIRECTORIES, MAGAZINES, AND INTERNET PUBLICATIONS. ■ BUILDING ON ITS LONG HERITAGE OF EXCELLENCE, THE COMPANY HAS BECOME GLOBAL IN SCOPE, WITH CITIES FROM SAN Diego to Sydney represented by Towery products. In all its endeavors, this Memphis-based company strives to be synonymous with service, utility, and quality.

A Diversity of Community-Based Products

Over the years, Towery has become the largest producer of published materials for North American chambers of commerce. From membership directories that enhance business-to-business communication to visitor and relocation guides tailored to reflect the unique qualities of the communities they cover, the company's chamber-oriented materials offer comprehensive information on dozens of topics, including housing, education, leisure activities, health care, and local government.

In 1998, the company acquired Cincinnati-based Target Marketing, an established provider of detailed city street maps to more than 200 chambers of commerce throughout the United States and Canada. Now a division of Towery, Target offers full-color maps that include local landmarks and points of interest, such as recreational parks, shopping centers, golf courses, schools, industrial parks, city and county limits, subdivision names, public buildings, and even block numbers on most streets.

In 1990, Towery launched the Urban Tapestry Series, an award-winning collection of oversized, hardbound photojournals detailing the people, history, culture, environment, and commerce of various metropolitan areas. These coffee-table books highlight a community through three basic elements: an introductory essay by a noted local individual, an exquisite collection of four-color photographs, and profiles of the companies and organizations that animate the area's business life.

To date, nearly 90 Urban Tapestry Series editions have been published in cities around the world, from New York to Vancouver to Sydney. Authors of the books' introductory essays include two former U.S. Presidents—Gerald Ford (Grand Rapids) and Jimmy Carter (Atlanta); boxing great Muhammad Ali (Louisville); Canadian journalist Peter C. Newman (Vancouver); two network newscasters—CBS anchor Dan Rather (Austin) and ABC anchor Hugh Downs (Phoenix); NBC sportscaster Bob Costas; record-breaking quarterback Steve Young (San Francisco); best-selling mystery author Robert B. Parker (Boston), American Movie Classics host Nick Clooney (Cincinnati); former Texas first lady Nellie Connally (Houston); and former New York City Mayor Ed Koch (New York).

To maintain hands-on quality in all of its periodicals and books, Towery has long used the latest production methods available. The company was the first production environment in the United States to combine desktop publishing with color separations and image scanning to produce finished film suitable for burning plates for four-color printing. Today, Towery relies on state-of-the-art digital prepress services to produce more than 8,000 pages each year, containing well over 30,000 high-quality color images.

An Internet Pioneer

By combining its long-standing expertise in community-oriented published materials with advanced production capabilities, a global sales force, and extensive data management capabilities, Towery has emerged as a significant provider of Internet-

TOWERY PUBLISHING PRESIDENT AND CEO J. ROBERT TOWERY HAS EXPANDED THE BUSINESS HIS PARENTS STARTED IN THE 1930S TO INCLUDE A GROWING ARRAY OF TRADITIONAL AND ELECTRONIC PUBLISHED MATERIALS, AS WELL AS INTERNET AND MULTIMEDIA SERVICES, THAT ARE MARKETED LOCALLY, NATIONALLY, AND INTERNATIONALLY.

STEVE DAVIS

◄ JONATHAN POSTAL

based city information. In keeping with its overall focus on community resources, the company's Internet efforts represent a natural step in the evolution of the business.

The primary product lines within the Internet division are the introCity™ sites. Towery's introCity sites introduce newcomers, visitors, and longtime residents to every facet of a particular community, while simultaneously placing the local chamber of commerce at the forefront of the city's Internet activity. The sites include newcomer information, calendars, photos, city-wide business listings with everything from nightlife to shopping to family fun, and on-line maps pinpointing the exact location of businesses, schools, attractions, and much more.

Decades of Publishing Expertise

In 1972, current President and CEO J. Robert Towery succeeded his parents in managing the printing and publishing business they had founded nearly four decades earlier. Soon thereafter, he expanded the scope of the company's published materials to include Memphis magazine and other successful regional and national publications. In 1985, after selling its locally focused assets, Towery began the trajectory on

which it continues today, creating community-oriented materials that are often produced in conjunction with chambers of commerce and

other business organizations.

Despite the decades of change, Towery himself follows a long-standing family philosophy of unmatched service and unflinching quality. That approach extends throughout the entire organization to include more than 120 employees at the Memphis headquarters, another 80 located in Northern Kentucky outside Cincinnati, and more than 40 sales, marketing, and editorial staff traveling to and working in a growing list of client cities. All of its products, and more information about the company, are featured on the Internet at www.towery.com.

In summing up his company's steady growth, Towery restates the essential formula that has driven the business since its first pages were published: "The creative energies of our staff drive us toward innovation and invention. Our people make the highest possible demands on themselves, so I know that our future is secure if the ingredients for success remain a focus on service and quality."

TOWERY PUBLISHING WAS THE FIRST PRODUCTION ENVIRONMENT IN THE UNITED STATES TO COMBINE DESKTOP PUBLISHING WITH COLOR SEPARATIONS AND IMAGE SCANNING TO PRODUCE FINISHED FILM SUITABLE FOR BURNING PLATES FOR FOUR-COLOR PRINTING. TODAY, THE COMPANY'S STATE-OF-THE-ART NETWORK OF MACINTOSH AND WINDOWS WORKSTATIONS ALLOWS IT TO PRODUCE MORE THAN 8,000 PAGES EACH YEAR, CONTAINING MORE THAN 30,000 HIGH-QUALITY COLOR IMAGES (TOP).

THE TOWERY FAMILY'S PUBLISHING ROOTS CAN BE TRACED TO 1935, WHEN R.W. TOWERY (FAR LEFT) BEGAN PRODUCING A SERIES OF COMMUNITY HISTORIES IN TENNESSEE, MISSISSIPPI, AND TEXAS. THROUGHOUT THE COMPANY'S HISTORY, THE FOUNDING FAMILY HAS CONSISTENTLY EXHIBITED A COMMITMENT TO CLARITY, PRECISION, INNOVATION, AND VISION (BOTTOM).

Library of Congress Cataloging-in-Publication Data

Knoxville : Smoky Mountain majesty / introduction by Howard H. Baker Jr. ; art
direction by Bob Kimball ; sponsored by the Knoxville Area Chamber Partnership.
        p. cm. — (Urban tapestry series)
    Includes index.
    ISBN 1-881096-92-0 (alk. paper)
    1. Knoxville (Tenn.)—Civilization. 2. Knoxville (Tenn.)—Pictorial works. 3. Knoxville
(Tenn.)—Economic conditions. 4. Business enterprises—Tennessee—Knoxville. I. Baker,
Howard H. (Howard Henry), 1925- II. Kimball, Bob. III. Knoxville Area Chamber
Partnership. IV. Series.

    F444.K7 K66 2001
    976.8'85—dc21

                                                                    2001023361

Printed in China

Towery Publishing, Inc.
The Towery Building
1835 Union Avenue
Memphis, TN 38104

www.towery.com

Publisher: J. Robert Towery **Executive Publisher**: Jenny McDowell **National Sales
Manager**: Stephen Hung **Marketing Director**: Carol Culpepper **Project Directors**:
Aleex Hopkins Conner, Connie Ledgett **Executive Editor**: David B. Dawson **Managing
Editor**: Lynn Conlee **Senior Editors**: Carlisle Hacker, Brian L. Johnston **Profile
Manager/Editor**: Sabrina Schroeder **Project Editor/Caption Writer**: Danna M.
Greenfield **Editors**: Jay Adkins, Stephen M. Deusner, Rebecca E. Farabough, Ginny
Reeves **Profile Writer**: Sharon Sweetser Pound **Creative Director**: Brian Groppe
Photography Editor: Jonathan Postal **Photographic Consultant**: Kenneth Smith
Profile Designers: Rebekah Barnhardt, Laurie Beck, Glen Marshall **Production
Manager**: Brenda Pattat **Photography Coordinator**: Robin Lankford **Production
Assistants**: Robert Barnett, Loretta Lane, Robert Parrish **Digital Color Supervisor**:
Darin Ipema **Digital Color Technicians**: Eric Friedl, Mark Svetz **Digital Scanning
Technician**: Brad Long **Print Coordinator**: Beverly Timmons

PHOTOGRAPHERS

A media entrepreneur and television producer, **Charlie DeBevoise** photographs small moments and quirky scenes throughout the Knoxville area for *Metropulse*, the local alternative weekly. He recently produced a documentary for The Learning Channel and cofounded an Internet site that provides counseling on-line.

Originally from Oak Ridge, Tennessee, **Roger Canada** specializes in landscape photography, primarily of the Smoky Mountains. He owns Roger Canada Photography, and his images have appeared in *The Flower Marker* and on promotional material for Key & Associates.

Specializing in nature and travel photography, **Kendall L. Chiles** owns Ken Chiles Photography and has had images published by several organizations, including the Smoky Mountain Visitors Bureau and Sealmaster Inc. He is a charter and board member of Southern Appalachian Nature Photographers, and serves as an instructor for the University of Tennessee Field School.

R.L. Doub specializes in images of nature subjects, scenery, outdoor action, and historical features and structures. His works have appeared on Hallmark cards and calendars, as well as in national magazines and numerous local brochures. He has received several awards from the Knoxville Dogwood Arts Festival and in a number of contests.

Originally from New Jersey, **Stan McCleave** owns McCleave Photography and has worked in Tennessee for more than 25 years.

Judi Parks is an award-winning photojournalist. Her work has been collected by numerous museums and public collections in the United States and Europe. Her documentary series *Home Sweet Home: Caring for America's Elderly* was recently honored with the Communication Arts-Design Annual 1999 Award of Excellence for an unpublished series.

Specializing in portraiture, **Karley Sullivan** is originally from Knoxville and works for Lifetouch Studios.

A freelance photographer with more than 17 years of experience, **Dan Tye** has traveled across the United States to photograph wildlife. He specializes in landscapes and nature scenes, and many of his photographs focus on regional points of interest in the Midwest.

As the chairman of the art department of Carson-Newman College, **David Underwood** specializes in fine art photography, and his works are included in the permanent collections of the Knoxville Museum of Art and the Asheville Art Museum in North Carolina. He recently completed a 20-year retrospective portfolio of black-and-white composite photographs, which resulted in an edited collection of 156 works.

The owners of Earth to Old City Giftshops/Galleries, **Bernadette** and **Scott West** specialize in fine art, nature, adventure, and travel photography, and have had images published in the Yellow Pages and on the covers of five newspapers. They have traveled the globe, selling thousand of images from their galleries and from their company Web site.

Other contributing photographers and organizations include Boehm Photography, Stephen Driver of Tennessee Children's Dance Ensemble, Jack Parker Photography, and the Women's Basketball Hall of Fame. For further information about the photographers appearing in *Knoxville: Smoky Mountain Majesty*, please contact Towery Publishing.

Knoxville

INDEX OF PROFILES

CASH
ADVANCES
AVAILABLE
HERE

DISCOVER
NOVUS
CASH NETWORK

VISA

MasterCard